# THE LAST PATROL

# THE LAST PATROL

FOLLOWING THE TRAIL OF THE ROYAL NORTHWEST
MOUNTED POLICE'S LEGENDARY LOST PATROL

## KEITH BILLINGTON

## CAITLIN PRESS

Caitlin Press Inc.
8100 Alderwood Road,
Halfmoon Bay, BC V0N 1Y1
www.caitlin-press.com

Edited by Betty Keller. Text design and cover design by Vici Johnstone. All images copyright Keith Billlington unless otherwise credited.

Printed in Canada

Caitlin Press Inc. acknowledges financial support from the Government of Canada through the Canada Book Fund and the Canada Council for the Arts, and from the Province of British Columbia through the British Columbia Arts Council and the Book Publisher's Tax Credit.

Canada Council Conseil des Arts
for the Arts du Canada

BRITISH COLUMBIA
ARTS COUNCIL
We acknowledge the support of the Province of British Columbia
through the British Columbia Arts Council

Library and Archives Canada Cataloguing in Publication

Billington, Keith, 1940-, author
     The last patrol : following the trail of the Royal Northwest Mounted
Police's legendary lost patrol / Keith Billington.
ISBN 978-1-927575-20-8 (pbk.)

     1. Fitzgerald, Francis J., 1869-1911. 2. Billington, Keith, 1940-
—Travel—Canada, Northern. 3. Royal North West Mounted Police
(Canada)—Biography. 4. Male nurses—Northwest Territories—Fort
McPherson Region—Biography. 5. Gwich'in Indians. 6. Canada,
Northern—Biography. I. Title.

FC3216.2.B55 2013          971.9'02          C2013-905060-4

# CONTENTS

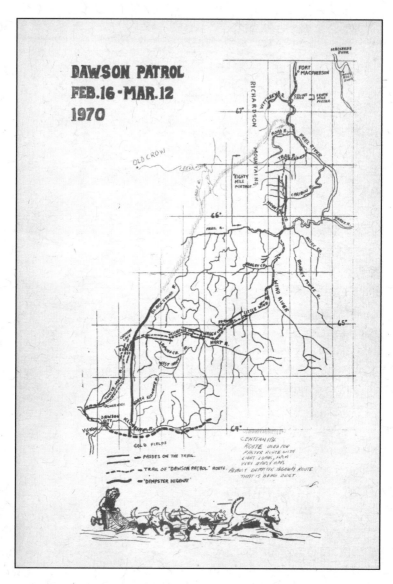

Centennial Project of Fort McPherson, 1970 route map. City of Dawson commemorative brochure.

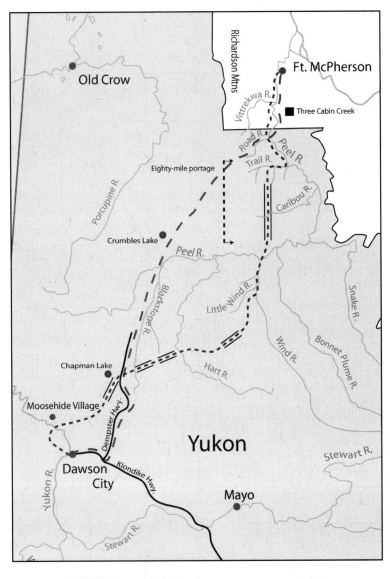

Richardson Mtns

Ft. McPherson

Vittrekwa R.

Three Cabin Creek

Old Crow

Porcupine R.

Eighty-mile portage

Road R.

Trail R.

Peel R.

Caribou R.

Crumbles Lake

Peel R.

Blackstone R.

Little Wind R.

Wind R.

Snake R.

Bonnet Plume R.

Chapman Lake

Hart R.

Dempster Hwy.

Moosehide Village

Yukon

Yukon R.

Dawson City

Klondike Hwy.

Stewart R.

Mayo

Stewart R.

- - - - - - RNWMP Dawson Patrol route

- - - - 1970 commemorative patrol route

———— mountain passes

↦
↦ portage route

# INTRODUCTION

The North has a special appeal for me because back in the 1960s I lived for six years in Fort McPherson in the Mackenzie Delta with my wife and two children, and during that time the Gwich'in people who live there endeared themselves to us. They have survived for thousands of years amid the rivers, lakes and mountains of an area that most people would find beautiful but inhospitable, especially in the winter, when blizzards, high winds, freezing temperatures and deep snows sweep over the land. I learned about their way of life when, as an outpost nurse, I travelled by dog team to their muskrat trapping camps and their caribou meat camps in the Richardson Mountains, and a number of times my wife, who is a nurse-midwife, and I camped, along with our young children, with the Gwich'in at their winter camps.

But it was while travelling by boat on the Peel River that we came upon a plaque on the riverbank marking the site where, in March 1911, searchers found the bodies of two of the men of the Royal Northwest Mounted Police "Lost Patrol." They had died of starvation and exposure while trying to return to Fort McPherson after an unsuccessful dog-team patrol that should have ended in Dawson City in the Yukon. A few miles upstream there was another plaque marking the spot where two more of the patrol's members died. The story of this "Lost Patrol" made world headlines in 1911, and as I stood looking at that plaque fifty years later it captured my imagination, too.

The indomitable spirit of such men has always intrigued me, and the question that often arises in my mind is: How would I have acted in the same circumstances? And I can feel the challenge rise within me. But Inspector Frances J. Fitzgerald, who led the Lost Patrol, was a leader of men. I'm not. I'm usually a follower, though when an occasion for adventure presents itself, I have tried to take advantage of it. I have been fortunate in these adventures to have been associated with men I trusted, usually my First Nations friends whose ancestors have travelled this country for so many centuries.

And so it happened that early in 1969 the government of the Northwest Territories began looking for projects that would typify life in the Territories in order to celebrate their centennial the following year. I sent a letter outlining my idea for a re-enactment of the Lost Patrol to show the close ties in the past between the NWT and the Yukon. I suggested that it should honour the Gwich'in men who had worked as guides and special constables with the RNWMP patrol system and provided much of the skill that was required for the members of the force to survive long trips in adverse weather and inhospitable terrain. I knew that this was an opportunity that shouldn't be missed because, once the Dempster Highway—which was already under construction between Dawson City and Inuvik—was completed, the trail that the RNWMP had followed between Dawson and Fort McPherson in the early 1900s would no longer be isolated and the opportunity to experience it as it had been would be lost forever.

This, of course, has come to pass. Today people rarely use dog teams and even the Gwich'in people hunt caribou from their trucks or snowmobiles. All the old guides who knew that route have died as have most of the men who accompanied me in 1970 on "The Last Patrol."

# UNFRIENDLY CLIMATE

As the small group of people stood around the four graves that had been dug with difficulty into the permafrost, five rifles were fired simultaneously into the frigid air in a military tribute to the four men they were burying. The graveyard in which they were laid to rest overlooks

This gravesite in Ft. McPherson marks the burial site of the four members of the lost Royal Northwest Mounted Police patrol.

Opposite: The peaks and rivers presented a confusing choice of routes through the mountains.

On a trip up the Peel River we visited the plaque that marks the site where Inspector Fitzgerald and Special Constable Sam Carter died during the fateful patrol. The marker is 32 kilometres from Fort McPherson. The plaque on the opposite page is another few miles south and marks the site where the other two members perished.

the Peel River, and to the west the Richardson Mountains stand out sharply in the clear air, but on this day no one was interested in the scenery. They were overcome by grief at the deaths of these men they had known so well. After a brief service, copper labels that had been locally manufactured were fastened to each of the coffins before they were lowered into the frozen ground and the volunteers were able to shovel soil over them. Then the mourners around the graves slowly broke up and made their way home to their cabins, all of them still feeling the shock of this tragedy that had occurred on their doorsteps.

In 1963—more than fifty years after that funeral was held on March 28, 1911—my wife and I came to live and work among the Gwich'in First Nations people in Fort McPherson as nurse-midwife

ON THIS SITE CST'S. C.F. KINNEY
AND R.D.H. TAYLOR, R.N.W.M.P.,
PERISHED FEBRUARY, 1911. WHILE
RETURNING TO FORT MCPHERSON
AFTER AN UNSUCCESSFUL ATTEMPT
TO PATROL TO DAWSON, YUKON
BY DOG TEAM.

and outpost nurse. One beautiful summer day on a boat trip up the Peel River we learned the story of the four men who had died. When we landed on a grassy riverbank, we found a large wooden plaque describing how at this site in March 1911 a search party led by Royal Northwest Mounted Police Corporal W.J.D. "Jack" Dempster had found the bodies of Inspector Francis Joseph Fitzgerald and Special Constable Sam Carter, who had perished on an aborted winter patrol from Fort McPherson to Dawson. We were told of another plaque a few kilometres farther up the river that marked the spot where the bodies of the other two members of that patrol had been found.

While in time we learned about many other deaths and narrow escapes from death in which the Gwich'in had been involved, the story of that Lost Patrol intrigued me the most. The reality of it was staggering. In 1910, forty-one-year-old Inspector Fitzgerald learned he had been chosen to be one of the men representing the RNWMP at the coronation of King George V, which was to be held in London on June 22 of the following year. To make sure he joined the contingent on time, he and his men set off from Fort McPherson on the annual winter dogsled patrol to Dawson City on December 10. The patrol's guide for the trip was Sam Carter, a former member of the force, who had travelled from Dawson City to Fort McPherson five years earlier and said he knew the way. The other two men were twenty-seven-year-old Constable George Kinney and twenty-eight-year-old Constable Richard Taylor. To make better time they were travelling light with just fifteen dogs, three sleds and only enough food for thirty days. But on January 12, 1911, having reached the Little Wind River, they were unable to find Forrest Creek, which would lead them to Dawson. Finally Fitzgerald had to concede that they were lost, and although they were more than halfway to their goal and had only four days' rations remaining, they elected to turn back to Fort McPherson. The return trip was made more difficult by extremely bad weather, and as their supplies dwindled, they gradually killed all their dogs for food. When the two younger men could go no farther, Fitzgerald and Carter went on in the hope of reaching help. The last entry in Fitzgerald's diary was February 5, 1911. With the exception of Taylor, all of them died of fatigue, starvation and exposure to the bitter cold.

During our six-year stay in Fort McPherson I drove my own dog team for hundreds of kilometres and learned to appreciate some of the experiences that had led to the demise of Inspector Fitzgerald's party, but I know that if it hadn't been for the education that I received while travelling with the Gwich'in, I could have met a similar fate. I am most indebted to our mentor, William Firth, the son of the renowned Hudson's Bay Company factor John Firth, who first taught us the rudiments of Arctic living, then enticed us to try it and never stopped encouraging us even when we failed.

And fail I did. The first time I travelled alone with my dog team on a routine medical trip to Arctic Red River, I was unable to correctly identify some of the lakes and portages (there were over thirty lakes to cross), and I spent the night sleeping in my dogsled. I did find my way out of my difficulties in the morning but was grateful to meet an RCMP corporal from Arctic Red River who had set out to find me, expecting the worst. Years later I suffered freezing temperatures when travelling to the Gwich'in caribou camps in the Richardson Mountains and endured the mind-numbing experience of facing gale-force winds when the temperature was minus forty degrees Celsius. On another occasion my friend Mike Wiggins and I encountered blizzard conditions on the last day of a three-day dogsled trip from Aklavik to Fort McPherson, but with all of these experiences I had not been hundreds of kilometres from home without food or shelter as the men of the Lost Patrol had been.

But long before I ventured by dogsled along the trails made by the Gwich'in, I flew over them while responding to urgent calls from the bush camps. It was a job that was challenging in the extreme, sometimes dangerous, and it nearly always provided me with an adrenaline rush that manifested in the proverbial "butterflies in the stomach." One winter day, with bush pilot Freddy Carmichael, I flew south up the Peel River to the Snake River to see a maternity patient, and I was awed by the vista below us as we approached the Wernecke Mountains to the south of Fort McPherson. Three major rivers cascade down from the southwest, the Snake, Bonnet Plume and Wind, all flowing into the Peel, and although modern tourist groups now canoe and kayak these exciting rivers, when I was there in the sixties, there was only one family living in all those thousands of square kilometres, although this had been part of the traditional land of the Gwich'in before they had contact with white men.

Although the land below us was covered with ice and snow, as we followed the valley of the Peel, we could see where it makes an abrupt turn to the west and is joined by the Snake, and from our elevation we could see even farther ahead to where the Bonnet Plume enters the Peel. But Freddy turned the plane eastward to the Snake River, and we began searching for the camp amongst the trees and creeks. And then there it was in a sheltered area by the river, only noticeable from the air by the plume of white smoke coming from the chimney of the family's wall tent.

The snow was incredibly deep, about a metre and a half, and landing the plane was no mean accomplishment. There was no marked strip, and we didn't know the ice conditions on the river, but Freddy was a skillful bush pilot and brought the plane to what I thought was quite an abrupt stop as the snow flew over us, whipped up by the prop. However, I already knew that the shorter the landing, the less likely we were to run into a boulder or a piece of driftwood. If the plane had been damaged, we would have had to crowd into the tent with the Gwich'in family until a search plane found us. After examining the patient, who refused my offer to take her with us to Fort McPherson to have her baby, thereby saving her a three-day dog-team journey, Freddy and I left the river with the snow blowing a blizzard behind us as we took off.

I realized then that Inspector Fitzgerald and his patrol would have passed close to this point on their way south to the Wind River, which joins the Peel about seventy-five kilometres beyond the mouth of the Snake, and I could imagine the effort it would have taken to break trail in this depth of snow even with good snowshoes. In deep snow if the tips of the snowshoes are not lifted as each forward step is taken, they plough into the soft snow and the momentum takes you headfirst into the snowbank. But constantly lifting your feet almost to thigh level is exhausting work, and having to do this hour after hour, day in and day out, is almost too much for a body to bear, especially when the temperature is far below zero and food intake is severely limited.

Reverend Isaac Stringer, who in 1905 became the Anglican bishop of Selkirk, which covered all of the Yukon as well as the Mackenzie Delta, spent almost forty years in the western Arctic, and he once said when referring to his earlier life in warmer climates, "I have often been asked how people coming from tropical climes could bear the rigours of the extreme Arctic weather, [but] it is really remarkable how human beings can accommodate themselves to various surroundings as they wander over the face of the earth." And it is true that after a while people do adjust to living in extreme temperatures, even to the cold of the North.

Most of the men of the Royal Northwest Mounted Police went voluntarily into this unfriendly climate to bring law and order to an area that was being devastated by whalers and hungry gold seekers, and by adapting to the ways of the First Nations peoples many of the force's members became very successful in their tasks and successfully travelled vast distances on patrol. Frances Joseph Fitzgerald was one who chose the North. He had started out as a shoe salesman in Halifax, Nova Scotia, but on November 19, 1888, he joined the North-West Mounted Police (later the RNWMP); he was nineteen. For the next nine years he served in Saskatchewan, but in 1897 he was recruited to accompany Inspector John Douglas Moodie, who had orders to make a trail from Edmonton to the Yukon River so that gold seekers heading for the Klondike would have a clear route to follow, one that could be monitored by the police.

Difficulties arose for the six-man patrol almost from their start in Edmonton, but as they made their way on horseback toward Fort St. John, life on the trail soon hardened them up. After struggling through the mountains they came down the Ospika River to the Finlay River and made camp near the Hudson's Bay store at Fort Grahame. As food was scarce there, some of the men were sent on to Fort St. James on

Stuart Lake to get supplies, but while they were gone, Fitzgerald walked back on their trail toward Fort St. John and collected supplies they had cached along the way. After wintering near Fort Grahame at a place still called Police Meadows, the party moved north.

They met several groups of men encamped at the point where both the Fox and Kwadacha rivers empty into the Finlay; it was at this location that Hudson's Bay built Fort Ware in 1927. As this was where the Kaska and Sekani First Nations people congregated annually, there were trails going out in every direction, but the NWMP troop took the main trail, known as the Davie Trail in honour of Sekani patriarch Aatse Davie, which took them north up the Rocky Mountain Trench to the Kechika River and on to what is now called Lower Post on the Liard River. They pushed north, then west, to Fort Sylvester, which had been built by Hudson's Bay on the Rapid River, a site that was to become known as McDames. By the end of that year the men, now trail-hardened and experienced in living in the bush, arrived at Whitehorse; the trip, which had been estimated to take three months to complete, had taken all of fourteen months. At Fort Selkirk on the Yukon River, Fitzgerald, who had begun the journey as a constable, was promoted to corporal and commended for his untiring work on the trail.

In 1900 Fitzgerald received a leave of absence from the force to join the Second Canadian Mounted Rifles and fight in the South African (Boer) War, where he served with distinction. On his return to the NWMP, he was promoted to sergeant and then became part of the contingent representing the force at the 1902 coronation of King Edward VII. Afterwards, he volunteered to go north again, this time travelling up the Mackenzie River to Fort McPherson by boat. From there he was sent with a Constable Sutherland to open a detachment at Pauline Cove on Herschel Island, a treeless piece of land in the Beaufort Sea, five kilometres from the Yukon mainland. The main task of the two men was to keep the peace among whalers and diminish the liquor trade, but Canada was also waking to sovereignty issues by this time, and the government was worried that Alaska might try to annex the island.

On the island the only shelter available for Fitzgerald and Sutherland was a pair of sod huts, but Fitzgerald fashioned furniture and other comforts from materials discarded by the whaling vessels. Fortunately, in 1906 they were able to move into an empty building belonging to the Pacific Steam Whaling Company, and this made their lives easier. However, it appears that Sutherland left around this time and was not replaced because in one of his 1909 reports Fitzgerald said:

> When there are no ships wintering at Herschel Island I think it is one of the most lonesome places in the north. There is no place one can go except to visit a few hungry natives. There is no white man to visit closer than 180 miles (290 km).

Besides the loneliness, Inspector Fitzgerald had to contend with the arctic environment. One December day the temperature dropped from minus five degrees Celsius to minus forty-five degrees in the space of five hours, and by midnight there was a howling blizzard, which blew the chimneys into the Beaufort Sea.

It is not really surprising that during his time on the island Fitzgerald had a serious relationship with a local woman, Lena Oonalina, and they had a daughter, born in 1909. Although he wanted the church to recognize the relationship and legitimize it, which the church was willing to do, he was told that the police force would not allow it. In fact, had the officials in Regina known of the relationship, Fitzgerald would have been asked to resign from the force as fraternization with local women was not allowed. He left Herschel in 1909 and spent a year in Regina, where he was promoted to inspector, but a year later he was happy to accept a posting back to the North, this time to Fort McPherson on the Mackenzie Delta.

By that time the easiest winter route to the Mackenzie Delta was the 764-kilometre overland trip from Dawson City by dog team, and every winter the Royal Northwest Mounted Police (the word Royal was added in June 1904) pushed patrols through the snow-choked mountains, visiting Native camps along the way and carrying mail from the "outside" to Fort McPherson, Rampart House, Herschel Island and Kittigazuit. If there was to be a personnel change in any of those detachments, the new officer would travel in or out with these patrols. Police journals show that by 1909 the northbound patrol carried about thirty-one kilograms of mail, which included some newspapers, but by 1916 they were carrying over forty-five kilograms of mail, which now included illustrated newspapers and six months of *Dawson Daily News* issues, all of which made quite heavy sled loads. During these patrols, the police and their Native guides suffered many hardships, deep snow, frostbitten hands and feet and accidents when they or their dogs fell through the ice, and there was frequently poor visibility in the mountains because of blowing snow and high winds. However, between 1905 and 1916, twenty-one patrols went over the passes without serious incident. The Lost Patrol in the winter of 1910–11 was the only unsuccessful patrol, and this was a major blow to the force.

It was a source of pride amongst the RNWMP patrollers to make the fastest trip between Dawson City and Fort McPherson. This was not a matter for official reports, though it seems to have been a well-known though unofficial contest. In fact, it was one of the similarities with some of the First Nations communities in which fast travel between certain points is still a subject for boasting, and perhaps it is a worldwide phenomenon: speed records are kept and boasted about, whether it is walking, running, cycling, skiing or driving, and beating those records is now a matter of fractions of a second. But for the men of the RNWMP patrols the time it took to travel between Dawson and Fort McPherson was really dependent upon the weather and the depth of the snow, and if the sleds were heavily loaded, it would certainly take longer.

First Nations people in the North are known to have walked hundreds of kilometres in all kinds of weather as a matter of course in their pursuit of game animals, berries and fish, and they went anywhere that would supply them with food for themselves and their families. For the nomadic Gwich'in people, caribou was the traditional source of clothing and food, and they followed the vast herds as they migrated north each winter to the calving grounds near the coast and then returned in the summer months. After gold brought Europeans to the North, the Gwich'in would periodically go to Dawson City to get basic supplies and then return to their nomadic existence. But Dawson saw a decline in activity and population in the early 1900s, and the Gwich'in found that, with the gold rush days virtually over, the town no longer held any attraction. Consequently the majority of this historically isolated group moved back into the mountains that had been their home for so many hundreds of years.

However, many of the young men who had seen Dawson City were now wise in the ways of the outside world, and compared with some of their people, they were quite flamboyant and frequently spoke about their experiences and travels. A number of them, among them my friend Andrew Kunnizzi, became known as the "Dawson Boys." This group knew the Richardson and Wernecke mountains and the Hart River area very well and frequently hunted caribou in these regions. But when it became apparent that fur was the new gold, the lure of good fur prices brought them and most of the other Gwich'in to the Mackenzie Delta, and Fort McPherson became their home.

Although death by starvation was fairly common in the North in those long-ago years, the whole area is full of stories of hungry white men who were saved from starvation and scurvy by Native people who rescued them. Consider the tale of George Mitchell, told in Angus Graham's book *The Golden Grindstone*. Mitchell was a Toronto insurance salesman who tried to get to the goldfields of the Yukon by heading north to the Mackenzie Delta and then south via the Peel River, hoping to get to Dawson via its headwaters. And he might have succeeded if he had not suffered an accident in the far reaches of the Peel, damaging his knee and putting a stop to his journey. This could have been the end of Mitchell if not for the Gwich'in, who not only found him but also treated his scurvy, performed successful surgery on his knee and eventually saw him safely onto a boat that would take him south again.

Two others who were saved from starvation were Anglican bishop Isaac Stringer and missionary Charles Johnson. In September 1909 they left Fort McPherson by canoe with provisions for eight days, planning to travel via the Rat River to the west of Fort McPherson, over McDougal's Pass and then via the Porcupine and Yukon rivers to Dawson. They had a guide who was to take them as far as Rampart House on the Porcupine River, but he left them without getting them that far. When the Porcupine began to freeze, they had to abandon their canoes. Their new plan was to walk to Lapierre House on the Bell River on the other side of the mountain divide, but they became lost and wandered for the next fifty-one days. They then decided to cut back across the mountains to the Peel River, and to sustain themselves after their provisions ran out, they snared ptarmigan and squirrels, then boiled and ate their sealskin boots. (As a result, Stringer became known as "the bishop who ate his boots.") When they encountered deep snow, they made snowshoes from spruce branches and continued their travels on them. At last they stumbled into a Native fishing camp on the Peel River but were so emaciated that they were unrecognizable. It was only when the bishop spoke that one of the Native people identified him by his voice.

The villainous figure known as the "Mad Trapper of Rat River" observed the local Native way of life and then adapted to it. Although he used the name Albert Johnson, no one knows who he really was, where he came from or what his background was; he turned up in Fort McPherson in July 1931, then built himself a tiny cabin on the Rat River. Six months later a Gwich'in man reported that Johnson was tampering with his trapline and the RCMP went to investigate. (I heard this story first-hand because the Gwich'in man whose trapline was tampered with was the father of Rachel Stewart, who worked for us in the Nursing Station, and after all those years he was still annoyed that Johnson had taken his traps!) After shooting and seriously wounding Constable Alfred King, who had confronted him at his cabin, Johnson fled into the mountains on snowshoes. Johnson led a posse through mountain valleys and over bare passes, and at one point in the chase he allegedly wore his snowshoes backwards to mislead the police. Trapped in a narrow gully he shot and killed Constable Edgar Millen and escaped again. Finally, with the aid of a plane piloted by the illustrious bush pilot Wop May, he was located near Old Crow in the Yukon. When he was shot and killed, all he was carrying for food was a single squirrel carcass found in his pocket, but knowing Gwich'in methods, he had managed to travel more than eighty-five miles in the three days of the manhunt.

A wolverine-trimmed parka kept my face quite warm when the wind chill was minus forty

# AN ARDUOUS JOURNEY

As part of my duties as an outpost nurse for the federal government I often travelled by dogsled into the Richardson Mountains to visit the nomadic family hunting camps. In this way I provided some basic health services, immunizing babies and young children, providing vitamins, removing decayed teeth and examining and treating those who were ill or quite often just worn out. These visits were frowned upon by my supervisors, who felt that the Gwich'in people should come to the village if they needed health resources. But living with the Gwich'in in their camps gave me valuable insight into their way of life, and every spring my wife, Muriel, and I would take our two young children and stay with families out in the mountains, in this way developing close relationships with many of the people.

Another of our responsibilities was to care for the health needs of the Gwich'in people at Arctic Red River, a settlement that has been known as Tsiigehtchic since 1984. It was a great place for me to visit because I made friends with an old man who lived there with his wife in a small house overlooking the Mackenzie River. Louis Cardinal was born in 1877 in what became Edmonton and he joined the NWMP when he was twenty. He became one of the force's best guides, especially on trips to and from Dawson City, and he had, in fact, guided the second-ever patrol from Dawson to McPherson in 1906. Whenever I visited Louis and his wife, Carolyn, he and I drank tea as he puffed on his aromatic pipe and I sat enthralled while he recounted his tales of adventure. He was such a good storyteller that in my mind's eye I travelled all over the North with him.

Louis had been part of the toughest summer patrol the RNWMP ever made, a three-man team that traced northern river routes all the way from Dawson City to Herschel Island. When travelling up the Blackstone River to the headwaters of the Peel—almost the same route that the dog teams took in winter—they often had to carry their canoe. They made innumerable portages and more often than not they were in waist-deep water as they pulled the canoe or held it back in the fast current. The Peel River gave them no rest with its whirlpools and canyons, log snags and submerged trees, but they arrived eventually in Fort McPherson before moving on to Aklavik and then Herschel Island. Returning was more difficult because they had to paddle against the current all the way to Fort McPherson. It was by that time almost September and freeze-up was imminent. Chief Factor John Firth advised them to stay in McPherson for the winter, but the Mounties were eager to get back to Dawson.

They travelled due west after leaving the Peel River, then paddled and pulled their canoe up the Rat River and into the Richardson Mountains, hoping to reach the Porcupine River before freeze-up, because the Porcupine would be their passage down to Lapierre House where they could catch a paddle steamer to Dawson City. It was going to be a 480-kilometre journey. As the team paddled and pulled the canoe, getting higher and higher into the mountains, the temperature began dropping rapidly, but they made it to Loon Lake at the summit and stopped for a day to dry their clothes. That night the sky cleared, the stars shone and the temperature dropped, and by morning Loon Lake was frozen over. They were stuck there for yet another day and Louis kept busy cutting and hauling firewood.

But the weather in the mountains can be quite fickle, and as luck would have it a chinook blew in, and the temperature soared as fast as it had plummeted. They climbed into their canoe and, smashing the thin, wet ice as they went, they reached the Porcupine River and rode down it, only to learn that the last paddlewheeler of the season had left the day before their arrival. Resigned to spending the winter at Lapierre House with the Hudson's Bay manager, they unloaded their gear. The next morning to their astonishment they heard the hoot of a boat whistle and, unable to believe their ears, they rushed outside. Apparently the steamer had struck a deadhead and the captain thought it advisable to return to Lapierre House to make the repairs before going on. While the repairs were being made, the patrol members stored their belongings on board, and the next day saw them on their way to Dawson City after making one of the most arduous summer patrols ever carried out.

Louis had also acted as guide on patrols to Herschel Island and east to Paulatuk in the Beaufort Sea north of Fort McPherson, west to Old Crow and the Hudson's Bay Company outpost called Rampart House as well as Lapierre House on the Porcupine River in the Yukon. He guided Charles Camsell on his surveying expeditions and saved various patrols from starvation by hunting meat for them when terrible mountain storms kept them holed up in their tents for days. He told me that in December 1910 he approached Inspector Fitzgerald and asked him to hold off on his fateful patrol to Dawson as he would guide him as soon as he had made a trip to Herschel Island and back. Unfortunately, Special Constable Sam Carter wanted desperately to make the trip to Dawson and convinced Fitzgerald that he knew the way. But Louis was concerned about Carter's knowledge because he knew how confusing the creeks could be up in the mountains.

In a situation very similar to that confronting Inspector Fitzgerald, Louis had been guiding two constables from Dawson City when they had to hole up in the mountains to wait out a windstorm. When katabatic winds whistle down the mountains, they can reach a velocity of hundreds of kilometres an hour. Shale and rocks fly by like shrapnel, and anyone in a tent risks having it blow away from overtop of them. My wife and I experienced such a wind when we were camped at Stoney Creek to the west of Fort McPherson, and the force of those winds was something that you had to feel and see to believe. Louis and his two constables were almost out of food when the winds came, and though they contemplated eating dog meat, they could not bring themselves to kill any of their dogs at that point. Taking advantage of the noise of the wind, Louis wrapped his parka hood around him tightly and made his way up the creek to where he knew there were several islands with good moose browse, hoping that he would find at least one moose sheltering there from the wind. He was either a very good hunter or just plain lucky, because he saw a moose on the first island. The moose saw him at the last minute and whirled around, but before it had even faced the other way, it had taken two bullets and fallen dead. Quickly he butchered the animal, cut out the tongue and the liver and returned to the camp to the surprised RCMP men, who hadn't even heard a shot. When they asked him how he had managed to get the moose, he just said, "Oh, he was just standing there." Louis laughed a short laugh at the memory and stopped to refill his pipe before continuing with his stories.

William Firth, who worked at our nursing station as janitor and handyman, was also a fount of knowledge about the North as he had lived there all his life. He was the son of John Firth, the renowned pioneer Hudson's Bay factor who had started out life in Stromness in the Orkney Islands and by strength of character had become a byword in Canada's north country. His stories of his boyhood in Stromness had obviously made an impact on William who, I am sure, felt that Stromness was his home, too, although he had never left Canada, and even some of John's accent had found its way into William's pronunciations. Over countless cups of coffee he told me stories and taught me how people survived in that rugged country.

Whenever I heard these stories about the Dawson trail from my First Nations friends in Fort McPherson and learned how they had lived in the mountains and still travelled through the valleys in their hunt for caribou, I could see that it held no fear for them. It was their backyard and they were as comfortable there as in a cabin in the village. However, it was the stories of the NWMP and tales about travelling over the mountains to Dawson City that kept me in awe, and I began to contemplate a dogsled trip to Dawson City with some of the Gwich'in men—if I could interest them in such a project.

Then I learned that Andrew Kunnizzi and Ronnie Pascal, two Fort McPherson elders whom I knew well, had made several trips between the two communities when they were young men. They had, in fact, snowshoed all the way from Dawson City to Fort McPherson to tell the people in the Mackenzie Delta that World War I was over, there being no other form of communication between the two communities back then, and they had felt that it was their duty to let others know what was happening in the great big world out there. This made me realize that these men were living history and their stories made me perk up my ears to learn more.

William Teya, George Robert and Fred Vittrekwa pause on the trail for tea and bannock.

# TIME FOR ACTION

The opportunity to do something concrete about initiating a commemorative patrol to Dawson City came in early 1969 when Jim Whelley, the general manager of the NWT Centennial Centre, announced via CBC Radio that the government was looking for ideas and projects that were representative of life in the Territories for the following year's centennial celebrations. So I thought, "Why not?" and, in a letter to Jim, proposed retracing the footsteps of the Lost Patrol. It was important for people to recognize the contributions the First Nations people had made to the history of the NWT and their long-standing collaborations with the police force.

Apparently there was a slow response to Jim Whelley's request for centennial projects, because my letter was one of the first to arrive in his Yellowknife office. I was quickly informed that if I would supply more details, the centre would look on my proposal with favour. I was elated, but now after all of the talking I had been doing, it was time for action.

I placed a poster roughly outlining the project on the village notice board, which was conveniently located in the vestibule of the Hudson's Bay store, asking if anyone was interested in the project. Some people laughed when they saw it, but a few of the young men put their names down immediately. However, after the project was advertised in more detail and people realized that the NWT government would be funding most of it, interest perked up considerably.

One big disappointment for me was that the RCMP brass told the local officers that they were not to associate themselves with the project. At first I could not understand why, but it was suggested to me that the force did not want to publicize the fact that the police had ever suffered a failure in their ranks. Furthermore, the RCMP was afraid it would leak out that Fitzgerald had a "country wife" with whom he had a child in 1909, a little girl named Annie. (I discovered later that Annie Fitzgerald had died in Hay River at the age of eighteen back in 1927.) So, although the local police were interested and helpful to me, that was all they could do—but I know that one member would have given his eye teeth to go along on the trip!

In working out the details for the trip, I used Inspector Fitzgerald's story as my guide to the amount of food for the men and the amount of food for the dogs, but as the Lost Patrol had starved to death, it would be necessary to go over this very carefully. We considered the possibility of resupply with wild meat, and then we had to decide on the route to be taken. Would we follow the police trail or would we go on the traditional Gwich'in trail, which used different creeks and mountain passes?

The only way to work things out properly was to get advice from people who had been on both trails, and although it had been perhaps fifty years or more since the men I talked to had been on these routes, things in the mountains and valleys would not have changed a lot. We decided that, in order to get things done, we should have a committee made up of village representatives, and though I wanted to be involved in the actual travel arrangements, it was better if we had someone who could look after the other arrangements and coordinate the activities with other First Nations villages and organizations.

The best person in Fort McPherson for this job was Neil Colin, an outgoing man who didn't mind saying what he thought. It was Neil who arranged to get summer caribou hides from Old Crow and then for women to tan the caribou hides to make parkas for the men of the patrol and do all the beadwork on the gloves and other articles. As other people got involved and began working together in the village, someone said that the people of Fort McPherson were doing what they wanted to: "Observing Centennial '70 in a most fitting manner."

When I spoke with Andrew Kunnizzi about the best route to take, I was delighted to learn that he was interested in making the trip himself, "just for old time's sake." Andrew was not a young man. In fact, he was seventy-eight years old, but he still drove his dogs to the Richardson Mountains and hunted caribou and travelled with his wife to their spring trapping on the Husky Channel in the Delta. To have someone like

Seventy-eight-year-old Andrew Kunnizzi agreed to join us on the patrol. He was the most experienced member of our patrol and had walked with Ronnie Pascal from Dawson City to Ft. McPherson to tell the people the First World War was over.

Andrew with the group would indeed be a bonus. He was of the opinion that the Wind River, the main route taken by the police patrols, was notorious for overflow. This happens when the rivers freeze down to the ground and the water from upstream floods over the ice, sometimes leaving long stretches of frigid open water, which can prove fatal for anyone getting accidentally submerged.

The other factor we had to consider was the time of the year to travel. Fitzgerald had set off in December, probably the worst time to travel as temperatures can dip to fifty or sixty degrees below zero or even colder in the mountains, and for most of the journey there would be very short days as at that latitude the sun does not show above the horizon between December 6 and January 6. The best time for travel in the Western Arctic is in the springtime, after mid-March when the days

A renowned hunter, William Vittrekwa loved his dogs and his dogs loved him and they would wait patiently for hours.

are much longer, the weather is clearer and temperatures have moderated considerably. On the other hand, if we set off on our patrol too late, then warm weather could overtake us toward the end of the trip closer to Dawson City, and travel by dogsled would be hampered by slushy snow or—if there was any delay en route—even a lack of snow.

As these discussions were going on, another very good friend of mine, William Vittrekwa, said he would like to join the re-enactment of the patrol to Dawson, and in his humourous way he let me know that I wouldn't get there without him. William had made the trip to Dawson a few times and said he could remember the way "easily." He and his wife, Mary, had been my hosts many times in the caribou hunting camps, and I knew him to be a strong and stalwart man. He was "about seventy-six or seventy-seven," he figured, but he could run circles around many men half his age. Once when I went hunting moose with him, I was unable to keep up as he followed a moose trail through deep snow. After I had slipped and slid down a riverbank that he had scaled on his snowshoes as if he were walking in the park, he told me, "More better you go back to camp."

One of the advantages of travelling in the North with remarkable old men like Andrew and William was that they had the map of the land etched in their brains. Of course, unlike returning to a city after many years of absence when you find streets and buildings have changed or been demolished, in the North the mountains, creeks and valleys don't change. Trees come and go but the geography stays the same. Most people in the North who make their living in the bush use visual points—rock formations, the junctions of creeks and rivers—to find their way. The closest things to signposts on the route are occasional lobsticks—trees with some of their branches cut off—that are used to show which creek to take or which lake to follow. Apart from that, it is the mountains that show the way.

About this time I was asked to attend a meeting in Yellowknife to discuss our plans along with people from other communities who were to present their proposals to Jim Whelley's committee. I flew from Fort McPherson to Inuvik on the regular scheduled Otter, transferred to the Edmonton-bound plane, which was always referred to as the "mainliner," and got off at Yellowknife. I found it invigorating to meet so many other people from across the North who had also come up with exciting projects to celebrate the NWT Centennial. I met such well-known people as the author and linguist Duncan Pryde, from the Eastern Arctic, who had been a Hudson's Bay store manager and travelled with and without Eskimo companions by komatik (the dog sled that the Eskimo used) and lived the Eskimo way of life. Later he served on the NWT Council for the eastern Arctic and authored the book *Nunaga*, which chronicled his adventures. Speaking with other northern old-timers made me feel like a novice and as if perhaps I had bitten off rather more than I could chew, but I was also encouraged because everyone was enthusiastic about my particular project, maybe because it went beyond the borders of the Northwest Territories and linked us with the Yukon. But maybe it was also because it had both historic and future aspects to it since it would follow the route of the proposed Dempster Highway.

Before I left for home, I was convinced that we, the people of Fort McPherson, could pull this project off, and at the same time I had that flutter of excitement in the pit of my stomach that I knew was caused by a mixture of adrenaline, fear and almost a dread of what I was getting myself into.

Back in McPherson, we began the task of picking the men who would make up the team to go on the patrol. This proved to be a bit of a headache as people signed up and then crossed their names off, then put them on again, and some who expressed a desire to go were not the most stable individuals in my estimation because of their histories of drinking or fighting. The fact that Andrew Kunnizzi was willing to go was the saving grace for the whole expedition, and I think that people felt comfortable with his sage advice. He had travelled the route since he was a small boy and knew the way, and that was important to me! In 1914 he had made a patrol with Sergeant Dempster, Charlie Rivers, Jacob Njootli and John Martin. At the time he had been staying at Black City, a camp north of Dawson, so he first travelled down to Dawson to start the patrol, guided the men to McPherson and back to Dawson and then returned to his cabin at Black City. Then in 1918 he and Ronnie Pascal had made the trip to Fort McPherson on snowshoes to bring word about the end of the war. Andrew had been one of the first men to speak with Albert Johnson, the "Mad Trapper of Rat River," and he recalled talking to him through the front door of his tent. And besides all of his other skills, Andrew was also a catechist in the Anglican Church.

William Vittrekwa, the other old man to volunteer, was the toughest old-timer in Fort McPherson and spent days and weeks travelling in the bush and in the mountains, especially in the upper Peel River area. He had a grand sense of humour, and behind his wrinkled face and rather toothless smile was a man whose knowledge of trails was unrivalled. He had been known to go out in mid-winter with his rifle and a thin grey blanket and be away for days in sub-zero temperatures hunting for moose. During one particularly cold spell he had spent every night with his blanket over him like a poncho, crouching over the embers of his fire; when daylight came, he was up and away. He had guided for a bit and claimed to have "cleaned all the sheep out of McPherson Mountain." He was also famous for having shot three caribou with one shot, but he would laugh and say that the last one got away on him! When William laughed, you could not help but laugh with him. He would pause for a moment just before he delivered his punchline, hold his hands up, then finish his line with a slap on his knees and a wide toothless laugh. Then he would pause again to see if he had got his point across and laugh again.

George Robert was a few years younger than Andrew and William, being only in his early sixties, and I was pleased when he said he wanted to be on the team. Even though I shuddered at the thought of anything happening to our two older guides, I knew that George would be a reliable man to see us through. He and wife, Annie, were generally quiet, neat people who spent a lot of time in the bush, though back in 1931 he had made a trip to Dawson City and worked there for a while as a longshoreman on the paddlewheelers *Whitehorse*, *Casca* and *Yukon*. George

George Robert was a man of many talents, having been a longshoreman then a trapper, and he was always in demand as a fiddler at community dances. George shot a moose to supply the patrol with fresh meat.

and Annie had children who lived "outside" or "down south." George was also a fine fiddle player and in great demand on dance nights.

We had decided that for practical purposes we would limit the number of participants to twelve at the most; otherwise the logistical problems, such as establishing food depots, would be unworkable. In an attempt to involve other communities, we asked if Arctic Red River would like to send a representative, and we did hear that they might send a man and his dog team if we scheduled the patrol after trapping season ended. With Andrew's assistance and recommendations we picked the other men from the list of those who had signed up and advised them that they had been successful in joining this "Last Patrol." They were Jim Vittrekwa, Fred Vittrekwa, William Teya, Peter

We relied a lot on Jim Vittrekwa for breaking trail in deep snow and for setting up camp.

41

The mail that we carried by dog sled from Fort McPherson to Dawson City was handed over to the Dawson Postmaster Frank Lidstone by Fred Vittrekwa.

Nerysoo, Abraham Koe and Abraham Vaneltsi.

Jim Vittrekwa was a good hunter and a tireless snowshoer, and he had good dogs, which was one of the requirements for our volunteers. He was also the acknowledged cook of the patrol. He and his wife had five children.

Fred Vittrekwa, Jim's brother, was one of the younger men on our patrol team. He had proved himself to be a strong worker, and

Lucy Rat watches Abe Koe from St. Matthews Mission House as he controls his dogs. Abe's lead dog shows his displeasure at the inactivity.

like most of the men he was a good hunter and could keep up with anyone on snowshoes.

William Teya was a good provider and hunter. He had been our guide on the first few dog-team trips Muriel and I had made to Arctic Red River, and he had been a member of the NWT Canadian Centennial cross-country canoe team in 1967 and gone all the way to Expo. His wife, Mary, was the daughter of Chief John Tetlichi and she had worked with my wife and me in the Fort McPherson nursing station.

William Teya was an excellent dog-team driver and had taken first my wife and then me on a trip to Arctic Red River.

They had two children. He had a pleasant personality and a soft smile; nothing seemed to bother him.

Peter Nerysoo, generally known by his nickname "Nayook," was a quiet man and another good hunter. Andrew said that Peter was a man that we could rely on for this trip as he had lived with his parents up near the Eagle River and might be able to remember some of the places we would be going through. When he was sixteen, he had travelled to Dawson City with William Vittrekwa and they had a very hard trip with deep snow and no game animals on the way. He was to be our patrol woodcutter. Peter and his wife had two children.

43

Abraham Vaneltsi was a young, tireless trail breaker who said he had "singing snowshoes." It was the mugs of tea that kept him going.

Abraham "Abe" Koe was an enthusiastic young man and tough as they come. He spent a lot of his time out in the bush or in his cabin down in the Delta with his wife and two children. He had a good sense of humour and seemed to fit in well with the others.

Abraham Vaneltsi, who was in his early twenties, was the baby of the group, but he had lived a hard life, caring for his older parents and supplying them with meat, wood and fish. He was used to travelling long distances with his dogs, trapping and hunting in the winter, and had become a very able man on snowshoes.

The tenth man was Bill Antaya, the Indian agent in Fort McPherson, who said he was part Cree although you would never guess it from his red hair. He also worked for the federal government as the area administrator for Fort McPherson and Arctic Red River. He and his wife had eight children. Bill was an enthusiastic supporter of the project and had quite a few resources to fall back on, and as things worked out personally for me, it was beneficial that he had joined the list of people willing to go. He had owned a dog team some years earlier and given them up, but in 1969 he accumulated a team of dogs again specifically for this trip, though he told everyone that he was only "an interested member" of the team. Bill and I were probably the least fit and experienced

Peter Nerysoo, "Nayook," had lived with his parents in the mountains and he recognized some of the places that we passed.

of all the men, but we were determined even while we both recognized that we would be depending on the others to get us through.

It went without saying that I was going to go and fortunately no one questioned my place on the team. In any case, I was ready to defend my position by pointing out that it had been my idea, and also I suggested, tongue in cheek, that if there were any accidents or illness, I would be a good person to have along. This seemed to be accepted without any problem. I was by that time thirty years old, an outpost nurse who, along with my wife, Muriel, had lived and worked in the Fort McPherson nursing station for six years and had grown to love the people. We now had two small children, both born in the Inuvik hospital and knowing very little about life "outside."

As well as all my dog-team trips to the rat camps and caribou camps on my own or with my Gwich'in friends, I had made a number of trips with Muriel and the children and a three-day trip with my friend Mike Wiggins. But I had also made two dog-team trips with members of the RCMP, once to the caribou camps with Constable Al Evans and once visiting the rat camps in the Delta with Corporal

Shane Hennan. The RCMP didn't use dog teams anymore and made all their local patrols by snowmobile, but the men who were posted in the North enjoyed working with the dogs, and whenever the opportunity arose, they would borrow a team from a family in the village and then accompany someone who had some experience. I felt privileged that Al and Shane had trusted me to take them to the various camps. Al and I had shared some exciting experiences travelling up frozen creeks and through overflow after dark, camping in windblown tents, which were more of a fire hazard than a shelter, and crossing mountain ranges where the wind could have blown us and our teams right off if our timing had not been right. My trip with Shane did not have any dangers attached, just long days and endless frozen rivers and frozen fingers, but we had been fortunate to be able to stay in trappers' cabins en route. With these and my other northern experiences behind me I felt that a five-hundred-kilometre dog-team trip to Dawson City was well within my capabilities, especially with some old, experienced Gwich'in men coming along with me!

Opposite: Bill Antaya took a few week's leave from his government post so he could make this historic journey. Bill was a redhead with freckles but was of Cree ancestry.

# THE DEMPSTER PATROL

As our plans progressed, we decided to call our patrol the Dempster Patrol rather than the Dawson Patrol because of the RCMP's reluctance to participate in the project. This name also paid tribute to the planned road from Dawson City to Inuvik via Fort McPherson, which was to be called the Dempster Highway. However, from force of habit we still referred to our project as the Dawson Patrol amongst ourselves.

We had by now decided that we would take the route used by the Gwich'in rather than the hazardous Wind River one, and this would also be more in line with the route proposed for the new highway. We would leave the Peel River at a tributary called Road River, travel over the mountains to Rock River, bear south to the Eagle River and continue south to cross the Peel again where it flowed from the west. From there we would travel down the Blackstone River to the North Klondike River, which would take us right to Dawson City. Sounded easy! Charlie Rivers, an old Gwich'in man from Dawson, told us later that the route we had chosen was for those "who didn't mind climbing mountains and had light loads." Fortunately I didn't know that when we set out!

Inspector Fitzgerald chose three men to make the patrol with him: two young constables, George Kinney and Richard O'Hara Taylor, and Special Constable Sam Carter, who at forty-one was the same age as Fitzgerald. Fitzgerald was familiar with a portion of the trail to Dawson City, and Carter said that he knew the rest of the way, even though he had only once taken the route from the south, four years earlier, and since then he had been travelling in many other parts of the North. In those days the force's patrols took an average of thirty days on the Dawson–McPherson trail, but it is not known whether Inspector Fitzgerald had estimated how long he was going to be on the trail. However, it is known that he wanted to travel light and fast, and consequently they took only basic rations, which consisted of the following:

- 408 kg of dried fish for the dogs
- 8 kg of candles
- 13 kg of tobacco

and foodstuffs weighing 161 kg (that is, 40 kg for each man), which included:

- 34 kg bacon
- 4.5 kg of corned beef
- 6.8 kg lard
- 1.3 kg salt
- 4.5 kg butter
- 9 kg of milk in tins
- 54.4 kg flour
- 6.8 kg dried fruit
- 13.6 kg beans
- 7.7 kg coffee and tea
- 2.7 kg baking powder
- 15.8 kg sugar

I found it interesting that although four men went on the patrol, they only took three toboggans and fifteen dogs, which was all of the dogs owned by the Fort McPherson RNWMP detachment. Apparently, one man would be expected to break trail with his snowshoes and help move the sleds up steep hills. It is estimated that each sled would have been carrying 272 kilograms, and this would have included their axes, rifles and cooking utensils. None of the sleds would have been equipped with a lazyback, which is an important equipment change since those days. This is a board with handlebars at waist height, which is secured about thirty centimetres from the rear of the sled and allows the driver to stand on the rear of the sled. The men in the early nineties didn't use this device because they didn't expect to ride on their toboggans; they either walked or jogged behind their teams.

By comparison with the supplies taken by the Lost Patrol, our Dempster Patrol seemed to have an overabundance of food, most of it donated by the Hudson's Bay Company, thanks to the Bay's manager, Dave Sullivan. Over the winter the following items were gathered together and stored in Bill Antaya's warehouse:

- 1360 kg commercial dog feed
- 340 kg corn meal
- 130 kg beef fat
- ½ case of candles
- 22.6 kg side bacon
- 11.3 kg oats
- 11.3 kg flour
- 5.4 kg coffee
- 10.8 kg tea
- 10.8 kg tinned butter
- 2.7 kg powdered cream
- 22.6 kg sugar
- 22.6 kg hamburger
- 1.3 kg baking powder
- 5.4 kg powdered juice

- 2.7 kg dried fruit
- 2 cartons matches
- 74.8 kg (bales) of dried fish

Besides all this, we were to carry three canvas tents, three stoves, axes, rifles and buckets for preparing the dog food. Andrew said that he, William Vittrekwa, Bill Antaya and I should each take an extra bale of dried fish for dog food.

We had one toboggan with lazyback per man and a total of sixty-seven dogs. We all carried good sleeping bags; mine was a Woods three-star bag, guaranteed to keep me warm to minus fifty-five degrees Celsius, but it was also quite heavy. The game warden also lent us a portable radio phone, which I think was offered in case we got into dire straits and needed to call for help. The officials really didn't want to see us become another lost patrol.

When we saw the amount of food piled up in Bill's warehouse, we were almost overwhelmed, so we decided to divide it up into three separate packs. Then, through the good offices of Great Northern Airlines and their pilots, we had one third packed into forty-five-gallon barrels to be flown out to a small lake called Crumbles Lake, then another third packed into barrels to be shipped to Chapman Lake in the Yukon. We divided the final third between the eleven teams that were to make the trip. (We were still hoping to hear if a representative from Arctic Red River would join us.) This arrangement meant our sleds would each be carrying at least 230 kilograms, not including our weight if we rode on the back. So much for the "light loads" that Charlie Rivers was to tell us about afterwards!

It was while I was in the middle of negotiating all these final details of the patrol that my private life almost interfered with my further participation. My wife and I had some time previously decided that we should move from Fort McPherson so that our children could experience some different aspects of North American life. This was brought home to us when on a quick trip "outside" our son saw some cattle in a field and thought that they were caribou. We also felt that we should move to another location because our professional lives were stagnating, and to be fair to the Gwich'in people, we should let new nurses come who would have fresh ideas and programs that would benefit the people.

So it was that in the fall of 1969, while we were in the midst of preparations for the last patrol, I was offered a new position in southern British Columbia and told I should be ready to move at any time. Muriel decided that this would be a good opportunity to take some time off to care for our children, especially as they would be in a completely different environment. The only life that they had really known was what they had experienced in Fort McPherson.

I wrote to my regional director requesting a leave of absence to go on the trip to Dawson. His gracious reply was that he would support me but that my request would have to go to my new zone director in Vancouver for full approval. I felt confident that with his backing everything would work out okay, but it did give me a shadow of concern.

Muriel and I and the children left for Vancouver in October 1969, but friends in Edmonton offered to accommodate Muriel and the children in the spring while I was up north on the patrol. As Edmonton had been our home for a year before we went to Fort McPherson, this offer made Muriel quite comfortable. For her and the children to stay in British Columbia would have been difficult because at that time she did not have a driver's licence, severely limiting her mobility. We made arrangements to drive back to Edmonton in time for the patrol, and the Centennial Centre in Yellowknife came up trumps after speaking with Pacific Western Airlines, which promised me a return plane ticket from Edmonton to Inuvik. With these concerns fairly well taken care of, I handed all the remaining material planning for the patrol over to Bill Antaya and took my dog team up to his yard where he would take care of them until I came back in the spring. I think that he planned to get his boys to feed the dogs and then begin running them as soon as conditions were right.

Andrew Kunnizzi was in charge of a bag of mail destined for Dawson City, including some letters to be sent to Canadian dignitaries around the world.

# ALL READY, BUT NOWHERE TO GO

With everything ready and Bill Antaya virtually watching the store, I left the North and moved to southern British Columbia. I thought that our children would have a hard time adjusting to living in this new environment, and I know that I certainly did. When we arrived in the south, it was October but there was no snow. Instead, the weather was humid and it rained frequently so that the ground underfoot was wet and muddy.

The people I worked for were all very pleasant, though I don't think they knew what my new position entailed. It had been made for me when I said that I would like to move south "close to the mountains," and I think that it was something like a reward for all the years that my wife and I had worked in the North. Perhaps not, but it seemed that way. I was to work on "special projects"—no one seemed to know what they were and I certainly didn't, but I went to work every day and tried to make myself useful. So it was something of a relief when February came and it was time to start out on the Dempster Patrol from Fort McPherson.

Dr. John Murie, my boss in Vancouver, gladly gave me permission to be away for up to two months—maybe he was glad to see the back of me already!—so, packing my old dog-team driving clothes into our Volkswagen, I drove our family to Edmonton where Muriel and the children were to stay with our friends while I was away. In our eight years of marriage I had been apart from Muriel for no more than two weeks at a time, and that was when I had been travelling in the mountains visiting the Gwich'in caribou camps. I couldn't imagine what she was feeling as I prepared to go off on a re-enactment of a trip during which all the previous participants had died.

On the morning of Friday, February 6, 1970, a friend drove our family out to Edmonton's Industrial Airport (now the City Centre Airport) to see me off. It was hard to say goodbye at that point, and I was glad that our friend had some other commitments to attend to and had to take Muriel and the children with her. As the car drove away, I felt very lonely and went to sit in the airport lounge to await the call to board the plane.

The morning was clear and the temperature hovered around zero degrees Celsius. As I walked toward the Pacific Western Airlines plane, a Javelin turboprop, I saw that Wally Firth was going to be on it, too. Wally was the federal government representative for the NWT and he was on his way home from Toronto. I was going to be staying at his parents' house in Fort McPherson, and it made me feel more comfortable seeing someone that I knew and could talk to.

Unfortunately, I didn't get to sit beside Wally. Instead I was seated next to a mountain of a man who was going north to be a Cat driver in Fort Simpson. He certainly looked the part of a Cat driver, and he took up one and a half seats, that extra half being mine. He was very pleasant and more like an overgrown schoolboy on an outing, and he was quite enthusiastic about this bit of travelling. Though I found it difficult to eat my lunch while my elbows were trying to fight each other for a place in my navel, the flight was enjoyable.

We stopped briefly at Fort Smith where I got out and stretched my legs—and arms—and after re-boarding, I enjoyed the luxury of having a whole seat to myself. As the plane flew toward Yellowknife, where the pilot informed us the temperature was minus twenty, I could feel my excitement increasing. The sun shone out of a cloudless blue sky, and I felt a surge of homesickness for the North and its beautiful spring weather, a far cry from the damp cloudy days that we had so far experienced in that area referred to as the Lower Mainland or the "Wet Coast."

On the runway at Yellowknife two gigantic Hercules transport planes were loading Nodwell Caterpillar tractors, and the tremendous noise made me long for the quietness of the real North. But my plane was not going to be flying to Inuvik that day so I had to stay in Yellowknife for the weekend. I spent my time reading, checking notes and going through my camera equipment to make sure I had everything that was needed and, most importantly, that it was all in working order. Then I met with two of the Centennial Centre men, Bob Baetz and Ted Boldt, to discuss my plans for the patrol in more detail.

The following morning I arrived at the airport to find that a wheel on the plane was being changed, and the passengers were all making up uncomplimentary names for PWA: "Please Wait Awhile" and "Pray While Aloft" and similar things. It was 4:30 in the afternoon before we finally arrived in Inuvik, and I got a taxi into town and stayed in the General Hospital staff quarters where I met some old acquaintances.

It was February 10 when I boarded the single Otter airplane for Aklavik and then Fort McPherson. The weather was foggy and the plane was cold; we were halfway to our destination before the heater suddenly came on, and all the passengers began to look a lot more relaxed. In many ways arriving in Fort McPherson was very strange: I didn't feel as if I had been away, as the people were all the same and greeted me like an old friend, but this time I was a visitor. It was not for me to go up to the nursing station and walk in and hang my hat. It was someone else's home now.

Instead, I walked up to William and Mary Firth's house, which was high on the riverbank overlooking the Peel toward the north and facing the Richardson Mountains to the west. After I greeted them like my long-lost friends, which they were, they showed me to the bedroom that would be mine for my short stay with them. Then over tea and bannock they filled me in on the local politics and gave me a quick account of where they thought the patrol plans were at from what they were hearing in the village. They told me that more people wanted to go on the trip, people who had laughed at us before but now wanted to be part of it because it was seen to be a prestigious event for the village.

When I left William and Mary's house after supper, I went up to see Bill Antaya, who was almost ready to throw up his hands in despair at all the changes that people were demanding. But a community meeting that night gave everyone the opportunity to air their feelings, and it gave me an overview of what was happening. We planned to leave in just under a week, which didn't seem very long when I thought of all the things that had to be done. The patrol members were finally confirmed as per my previous list except for one man, George Neditchi from Arctic Red River, who had been invited to join as a representative from that community. We had heard nothing from him and we had to conclude he would not be coming. Later Bill and I pored over the maps, and it was only then that it dawned on us that we were going to be travelling a long way through country where no one lived anymore and where stories abounded of hardship and deprivation. We looked at each other, then laughed, and Bill said, "Well, what the heck! Let's have another coffee!"

I finally got to bed at two in the morning with my thoughts rushing from one item to another. It was visions of desolate mountain vistas that finally put me to sleep.

Inspector Fitzgerald's patrol had consisted of four men, three sleds, fifteen dogs and enough food for thirty days. We had eleven men, eleven sleds and sixty-seven dogs, which meant six dogs apiece except for Peter Nerysoo (Nayook), who always used seven dogs in his team, although he said he would manage with the same allotment of dog food as the rest of us. With the food we would be carrying and that we planned to cache along the way, we were in no doubt that we had enough food for a month. In addition, the men hoped to kill an animal—a moose or a caribou—along the way to give us fresh meat and to stretch out our supplies. Knowing that my blood sugar would probably run low if I was exerting myself for long periods, I packed a box of chocolate bars and some packages of barley sugar. I just had to remember that these were *emergency* rations!

Helen Sullivan, the wife of the Hudson's Bay manager, was busy sewing my dogs the fancy dog blankets that were the traditional "dress-up" for the teams. Added to this were the matching dog irons, the large pompoms that were wired to the dogs' collars so that they stood up about fifteen centimetres above their heads. Mary Firth was putting the finishing touches to a pair of mukluks that she had been making for me and had just completed a caribou-skin parka in the style that the Gwich'in used at the turn of the century. Meanwhile, the women of the village had been making the same fashion of parka for the other men and making themselves dresses that reflected the styles of those early days.

The traditional parkas for the patrol members were made by the Gwich'in women out of the summer caribou skins from Old Crow.

For the parkas, the Gwich'in people of Old Crow (the Vuntut Gwich'in) had sent over summer caribou skins because they are darker in colour and have shorter hair than the winter skins. They were tanned locally and then sewn with sinew and given a lining of cotton. These parkas were roomy and tied around the waist with a sash. Caribou hide with white hair was used on some of the parkas to make a design around the hem. Our mukluks were again in the traditional style, just like the everyday mukluks that the Gwich'in wore—canvas tops that came to just below the knee where they were tightened with wool toggles. The bottom portion of the mukluk or "shoe" part was soft moosehide with thong laces sewn into the back by the heel, and these laces were wrapped around the ankle and tied in front like a shoelace. The Centennial Committee in Yellowknife had sent us duffle hats that had been made for the celebrations, and we each sported one of these with the centennial emblem and a pompom on top.

Neil Colin had planned a community dance for an evening just a few days before we were due to leave, and everyone turned up in period costume. The women were in colourful long dresses, and those of us who were going on the patrol had to wear our caribou-skin parkas and centennial hats. The community hall was packed and hot, and I felt quite shy, which was only exacerbated when the first dance was called and they hollered for me as the patrol leader to take the first dance. This, of course, was a jig, a dance the Fort McPherson men, women

Carolyn Kay and Andrew Kunnizzi show off their turn-of-the century costumes worn at the community dance.

The first dance of the night was a robust jig, and Mary Firth (above) was my partner. Everyone wore period costumes, but the men of the patrol had to wear the caribou-skin parkas and centennial hats. We were a bit warm.

and children are famous for. Charles Koe played the fiddle and there was someone with a guitar to strum, which was all fine except that I had almost forgotten how to dance the jig. I had never been good at it, mind you, but I had always managed to shuffle around a bit trying to get my feet to do the intricate footwork, and now here I was in front of all my old friends at it again. Mary Firth was my partner and she did really well between fits of giggles, which were echoed throughout the hall, but finally it was over and I retired to the sidelines pouring with sweat. Some of the men who were going on the patrol had a few too many drinks, and I hoped that they would soon be over it because we were to pack up and leave within two days.

On Friday, February 13, things came to a head, and after having some serious discussions about whether we had too much or not enough dog feed, we figured we would go with what we had. Perhaps the dogs sensed the excitement that was building, especially when we were looking at the dog food, because my lead dog, Silver, got into a fight with another dog that just happened to be sniffing around, and Silver was bitten on his right front paw. I could see that the flesh was torn and Silver could not put his weight on it.

I was chagrined. I did not have a spare lead dog and Bill and I were in a bit of a quandary. I poured out my tale of woe to the Sullivans as I was eating supper with them in the Bay house, and Helen volunteered to make some dog booties for Silver. These were something he had never worn, but I had heard that dog mushers in Alaska used them frequently when their dogs were travelling over ice. I went to the nursing station and begged a few cc's of intramuscular procaine penicillin and a disposable syringe, which they gave me willingly once I explained it was for my dog. I gave Silver half of a syringe of this long-lasting penicillin and hoped for the best.

On the next day, Saturday, Bill and I waited around for the plane that was to take our first cache of food out to Crumbles Lake, but the weather was so poor that even if the plane had made it to Fort McPherson, it would not have been able to get to the mountains. Then we called round to Andrew Kunnizzi's house to pick up a bale each of the dried fish we were to carry for our dogs. William and Mary Vittrekwa had set nets out in the summertime, and after filleting the fish and drying them in the wind and the sun, they had baled the fish in bundles and stored them in Andrew's shed for safekeeping. On the trail the dried fish had to be soaked in water for a short time before feeding the dogs, and along with this they were given a half block of beef fat. The dried fish was good in that it was light to carry, but it was quite bulky compared to the packages of Miracle dog food, a mixture of oats and other cereals along with "meat by-products," on which the dogs thrived. But a side benefit of the dried fish was that we could always eat it ourselves if we were in dire straits—I couldn't really contemplate eating my dogs.

Sunday, February 15, dawned foggy and freezing, with the temperature around minus forty degrees, and all the patrol members were asked to do a sort of dress rehearsal of our leaving so that the film crews could get the shots they wanted. Mike Zubko, a pilot from Inuvik whom we knew, came to take pictures of me hitching up my dogs and filling the sled with supplies. Then we drove our dogs down to the Peel River where we waited around while more photos were taken, and at this point some of the dogs, all excited but with nowhere to go, got into a fight that warmed up the owners as they waded into them with whips and boots to prevent them from tearing each other apart. But the riverbank was crowded with people who had come out to see us and they were all enthusiastic, which made us feel good.

That evening I was invited out to supper again at the Sullivans', but when I went down to the Firths' house to get ready, Mary told me that she had made a special supper for me and that it was ready. Not wishing to snub anyone, I did what I thought was best—ate supper with William and Mary, then about an hour later walked up to the Sullivans' where I ate another supper. That night I waddled home quite replete but feeling sorry for the dogs that were going to have to pull the added weight the next day.

The dogs were hitched in tandem to make it possible to manouevre around trees. They were fed only at night but could travel all day, up to 80 kilometres with a full load. It was the only transportation that the Gwich'in had between October and June.

# MILES TO GO

Inspector Fitzgerald left Fort McPherson on December 21, 1910, without fanfare. After just a brief handshake and a salute the men had pulled out of the village and onto the Peel River. Our leave-taking would be just the opposite. Television crews and dignitaries from different agencies were all descending on Fort McPherson to make speeches and to wish us well. I think that some people, locals included, were convinced that this was going to be another lost patrol and didn't really expect to see us again. Just in case that happened, some of them went the rounds trying to collect our autographs.

The big day arrived and I was feeling a bit cold with anticipation. What if some of the men had been drinking? What if Silver's foot was too damaged for him to go? What if my sled tipped over in front of the community members and the cameras only got a shot of my rear end as the dogs pulled me over? With all these thoughts racing through my head and a lot more besides, I glanced at the thermometer: minus forty-seven degrees Celsius with a wind chill factor of minus sixty-five degrees! Normally we would have postponed our departure in such weather, but with all the hoo-ha that was going on we couldn't wait for another day. Fortunately—in some ways anyway—we had to wait for all the ceremonies to be over before doing our final packing, but it didn't seem to get any warmer as the day went on.

By mid-morning we all dutifully congregated in the school

auditorium where a large crowd was gathered, and everyone waited for speeches by the visiting dignitaries. Neil Colin was the master of ceremonies: as a local man he excelled in getting and keeping control of the crowd, and he had a great sense of humour. Looking around, I was surprised to see some of the people who had come to see us off, considering their attitudes at first. They included Inspector C.J. Dent, who had come to represent the commissioner of the RCMP. As I looked up at him on the stage, I couldn't help thinking how different he looked from how I imagined Inspector Fitzgerald would have looked. Fitzgerald had worked in the field, whereas Inspector Dent was obviously a desk policeman.

Jim Whelley was there to represent the commissioner of the Northwest Territories; Alex Gordon represented the regional director, Inuvik Region, Government of the Northwest Territories; Mr. R. Morrison represented the Northwest Territories Centennial Centre. But the people I was most delighted to see were Louis and Carolyn Cardinal, my old friends from Arctic Red River, who had been flown over to Fort McPherson in the RCMP Otter. Louis was now ninety-three years old and he stood on the stage supported by Inspector Dent. He made a few remarks, and though it was very difficult for him as the large building and the bright lights were strange to him, he faced it all bravely while Inspector Dent supported him with one arm—which was quite fitting because Louis had spent his life supporting the force.

Next to speak was Ronnie Pascal, the man who had walked from Dawson City on snowshoes with Andrew Kunnizzi in 1918. Ronnie spoke for a few minutes about the old days and wished us well, probably thankful that he wasn't going anywhere on this freezing cold day! Both Andrew Kunnizzi and I were asked to say a few words, and they were certainly just a few because we had a lot to do before we got underway. We had our photographs taken with the women who had sewn our caribou-hide parkas and who had made themselves the beautiful long and colorful old-time dresses. Then as we were leaving, a sack of mail was handed to us to take to Dawson, and we asked Andrew if he would be the official postman.

Afterwards, the patrol members rushed to their homes to pack their sleds and harness their dogs. Bill and I did the same, only we decided that Bill would drive his dogs north down the village road to where I would be waiting at the Firths' house, and from there we would take the less steep trail down onto the river, thus avoiding embarrassing spills. We would meet up with the others at the bottom of the main trail from the village. This manoeuvre may have spoiled the filmmakers' idea of what the leaving should have looked like, but we thought that it would work quite well for us novices.

One of William Firth's grandsons helped me to load my sled by carrying my supplies out of the house, and then I packed the sled so that I knew where everything was. I had a really good oak toboggan that was about four metres long and I used a moosehide wrapper, a sort of long, deep bag into which my supplies went to keep them from falling into the snow. I used a canvas cover over the whole load and lashed it down tightly, then as a last flourish I fastened my rifle in its embroidered moosehide case underneath the snowshoes that lay on top of the load so both would be readily accessible. It seemed fitting that my large birch snowshoes had been cut and fashioned by Ronnie Pascal, and his wife, Laura, had been the one to cut the fine babiche for Ronnie to sew the bindings. I wrapped a beaded bag containing shells and matches and a few other personal items around the handlebars of the lazyback and stashed my axe handily in the loose part of the carriole behind it. This was also where the dog chains were kept as they would be the first things required at the end of the day.

Finally I harnessed up the dogs, who were eager to go, and they barked excitedly, tugging at the traces which I hoped would take the strain, because they were going to be thoroughly tested by the end of the trip. By the time this was all done, my fingers were freezing because I couldn't fasten the traces and the sled wrappings with my big mitts on, and I had to keep putting my hands into my armpits to warm them up. I moved the sled slightly and my heart sank. It must have weighed more than the 230 kilograms that I had estimated. I worried that I wouldn't even get out of the village with this lot.

I examined Silver's foot, and as it still looked a bit raw, I gave him the last of the penicillin and tied the leather booties that Helen

I finished packing my sled with everything but the kitchen sink. The tent stove made my dogsled look top heavy. I was now ready to hit the trail from William and Mary Firth's house.

Sullivan had made onto his feet. He sniffed at this new piece of equipment, then promptly ate the boot right off his injured foot. As he did not seem to be limping as much now, I thought I'd let him go with it as it was and see what happened.

Bill arrived at 1:30 p.m. and I told him about my heavy load. "Don't worry," he said. "I think everyone is going to be the same. I could hardly move mine but when I got out onto the road, the dogs just flew down here!"

I got my dogs all lined up and went ahead of Bill, calling out loudly "Okay!" to the dogs, and Silver immediately tightened the traces. I untied the headliner rope, which had been holding the sled back,

Jane Charlie watches over a loaded dogsled as other community members gather to wish us farewell.

and the dogs gave one heave and we were away with Bill following hot on my heels. We drove the dogs down to the river in a shower of ice crystals as our sled brakes dug into the icy snow, but when we reached the river, we slackened the pace and drove the half-kilometre south to where the others would be coming down onto the river.

The temperature down on the Peel River was another ten degrees colder than it had been in the village, and I was surprised and delighted to find that my caribou-skin parka was really quite warm as underneath it I had only a thermal vest, a wool shirt and a sweater. I had woollen gloves inside my big wolf gloves, the latter always excellent for covering my face when I was travelling into a biting cold wind.

As soon as we had assembled on the river, we glanced up at the riverbank in front of the village and saw that it was lined with waving people who had braved the cold to see us off. We waved back and set off southward up the Peel, following a dog-team trail made by hunters and others heading for their cabins. My dogs seem to be pulling slowly and I jogged behind them, thinking that I was going to be at the tail end of the patrol all the way if they continued like this. Maybe my load was too heavy? I didn't think that I had brought too many extra things with me, things that the others wouldn't have. I had a big roll of maps, a movie camera and two still cameras and a good supply of film. I had a pillowcase half full of bannock that Mary had made for me at the last moment, and oh yes, I had that bag of Mars Bars just in case of emergencies because I really didn't want to follow in Fitzgerald's footsteps.

We stopped at a small island a few kilometres upriver from Fort McPherson near a place called Shiltee Rock, where there is a shale outcropping that provides a good landmark. All the dogs lay down panting. As usual they had started with great gusto but soon slowed down, though they were pulling the heavy sleds without too much difficulty. As they lay there biting off great mouthfuls of snow to slake their thirst, I could not help feeling happy to be out with them again. I had missed the excitement of running dogs while I was in the south.

I had a good-looking team, three of them being the large grey-and-white Siberian crosses I had got from the RCMP when the police had a dog-breeding station at Arctic Red River. Silver, my leader, and Adaijoh (or "Whiskers"—named after me) had been with me on many

William Teya drives his dog team past the Northwest Territories flags as community members line the riverbank to see us off.

The dogs were not the only tired ones on the first day. Bill Antaya sits and ponders what he has committed himself to!

trips and they were good workers. One young dog was named Friday because I had got him on a Thursday along with his brother who was, of course, called Thursday. (My imagination must have been stalled that day.) Another of the dogs, the one I called Easter because that is when he came to me, I used in the wheel-dog position next to the toboggan. He was also a former RCMP Siberian and had come over from Old Crow when the police made a last dog-team patrol over the mountains. He had refused to run down the mountain slopes and been dragged so that the pads on his feet had been virtually scraped off. As a result, he had been left in Fort McPherson to be put down. The RCMP, being a federal force, could not give government property away, so a sentimental officer suggested that they shoot the dog on paper and give him to me. I had kept Easter tied up until the next season and then had broken him back into his traces by going short distances until he was as good as my other dogs, but as he was a stranger to the team, I put him in the wheel-dog place so the other dogs would not gang up on him. The two dogs that did not fit into the colour scheme were ones that I had bought from Old Lucy Rat when they were pups. One of them I frequently called Ginger because he was, but his given name had been Nicki; the other who had brown markings instead of grey I called At-tuk, and he was the only one that would go looking for a fight.

The men soon had a large fire going and we had tea and some lunch because we hadn't had the opportunity to stop and eat since breakfast time. Some fried moose meat and scalding hot tea soon revived me as I am sure it did the others, and a short time later we set off upriver again, feeling that now we were really starting our trip. The dogs worked better after their short rest and quickly got into their mile-eating pace.

# SOUTH WIND

When Inspector Fitzgerald left Fort McPherson on December 21, 1910, the temperature had been minus thirty-two degrees Celsius. It was snowing but the wind was from the north and therefore behind them so they did not feel the cold. At that point the Peel River, which they were following, is about ninety metres wide, and like most rivers entering the Mackenzie Delta it winds lazily along the flat land. However, farther south where the river comes down out of the mountains, it is much narrower and birch and spruce cover the banks. There was not much of a trail to follow.

In the late 1800s and early 1900s the Gwich'in people spent most of their time in the mountains and Upper Peel areas where the huge caribou herds were to be found. When supplies were needed, those hunters who were in the upper reaches of the watershed would travel to Dawson City or Mayo rather than head north to Fort McPherson. Consequently, the only trail for the patrol to follow on that December day had been made some time previously by a RNWMP officer who had cached dog food at Trail River in preparation for Inspector Fitzgerald's patrol. However, this trail was soon obliterated by the falling snow, and the going got steadily harder. Inspector Fitzgerald wrote in his diary that due to the difficulty in breaking trail they only managed to go twenty-four kilometres that day.

The travelling was made easier for Fitzgerald and his men on the second day when the wind shifted to the south, and it also became a little warmer. Men and dogs worked hard and there were no problems. Now the trail they were still following had blown snow on it, but the route so far was familiar to each patrol member and their spirits were high.

Unfortunately, these good conditions did not last into the next day. The south wind soon raised the temperature to minus twenty-three degrees, bringing mist with it. On Christmas Eve it snowed heavily and they were only able to make twenty-five kilometres.

In four days the patrol had covered a mere 106 kilometres. They passed Colin's cabin and in midafternoon came upon an old Indian camp. By now the dogs were tired after plowing through the new snow and the men, equally tired from breaking trail on their snowshoes, were hot and needed a rest. Inspector Fitzgerald decided to make camp early and they busied themselves finding and cutting dry wood for the stove and evergreen brush for the tent floor. After the tent had been set up, they fed the dogs, ate their own supper and turned in early.

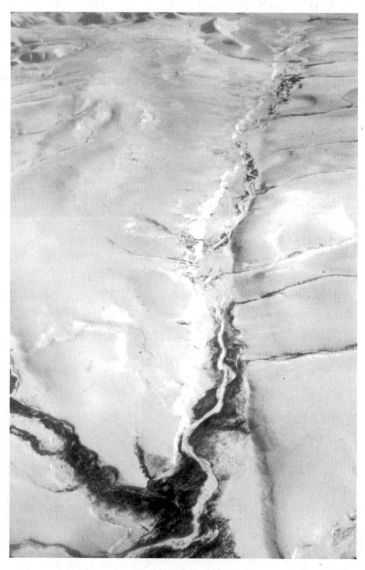

The river snakes its way into the barren mountains where strong winds blow relentlessly.

# QUIET AFFAIR

After leaving the island where we had stopped for lunch, the dogs worked well. My dogs, although slower than some of the teams that had been used for long trips into the mountains only weeks before, did not lag behind too far. As long as they could see a team ahead of them, they pulled with a will.

Travelling by dogsled is a fairly quiet affair. There is no one to talk to and I had learned not to talk to the dogs as I was travelling after

Peter Nerysoo has his dogs in perfect control as he wends his way up the Peel River.

an old Gwich'in man told me that if I talked or whistled or made chirping noises—all of which I used to do to remind the dogs that I was still there—they would not hold their attention to the trail. The silence was really quite rewarding. The panting of the dogs and the creak of the oak toboggan on the hard-packed, snowy trail were themselves something to savour, and when I jumped off the back of the sled, which I had to do periodically to keep warm, the pounding of my mukluks on the snowy trail was soon drowned out by my heavy breathing. When I jumped back onto the sled again, some of the dogs would look around at me with what I thought was disdain—or was it disgust? Who did I think I was, adding to their burden? The trail went up the middle of the river so all there was to see were the spruce trees on the riverbank, and beyond them about half a kilometre away were the hills covered in the short spruce and willow that are so common along that stretch of river.

Time for a night's rest in Brian and Lucy Francis's cabin at Vittrekwa Creek. Peter Nerysoo, George Robert and William Teya find sleeping room on the cabin floor.

At 5:30 that afternoon we arrived at Brian and Lucy Francis's cabin near the mouth of Vittrekwa Creek, and I noted that we had travelled thirty-two kilometres in four hours. After we chained our dogs to the surrounding trees and bushes, we put down a few spruce boughs for them to lie on, and as soon as their beds were made, they circled and plonked themselves thankfully down.

Although Brian and Lucy's cabin was quite large, when we spread ourselves out, there was not too much room to spare. Abe Koe made a large fire outside and several of us melted buckets of snow and heated the resulting water so that we could mix up the feed for our dogs, each man looking after his own because none of us trusted anyone else's dogs. Supper was a shared meal of fried moose meat and bannock cooked up in one of Lucy's large fry pans, and afterwards we looked around to decide where to lay out our sleeping bags. There was one wooden bed in the cabin and everyone insisted that I use it, which was rather embarrassing, but they obviously thought that being a white man and their so-called patrol leader I should have this bed. I tried to convince Andrew or William to take it, but they both shook their heads and said that they were used to this kind of life and I wasn't. Bill could not be convinced to take it either, and I knew that he was quite tired too, so with some reluctance I unrolled my sleeping bag and made myself as comfortable as I could. Of course, the bed had no mattress, just rough-cut boards that were as hard as the timbers on the floor where everyone else would be sleeping, so although I had an elevated bed, it could not be defined as anything luxurious. I fell asleep thinking that—amazingly—here we were on our way to Dawson. It didn't seem quite real, but in the darkness the heavy breathing of the men soon lulled me off to sleep. I woke several times in the night and tried to find a soft place on the hard bed, then consoled myself that it would be softer sleeping on a bed of boughs later on when we were in tents.

Early on the morning of our second day, February 17, I heard someone stirring followed by the sound of a match being struck, and soon the reflections of stove flames were dancing around the cabin. A couple of candles were lit, and the room became a hive of activity as bedrolls were tied up and the clank of metal plates and teakettles announced that breakfast was under way. The large fry pan was again put to use, and we started our day with hamburger and beans followed by large mugs of tea. I ladled some sugar into my tea as I was sure that I was going to need the extra energy.

I had thought there might be some reluctance among the men to get up early in the morning, but perhaps because Andrew inspired us, everyone was up and eager to go, even though it was dark and we had to use candlepower to see by. We all got organized quickly and dashed

Early morning travel on the river ice was bitterly cold but it was beautiful—if you could keep warm.

outside to have a quick wash in the snow—and I mean it really was a quick wash with only hands and face honoured. As soon as I stepped out of the cabin, the cold air made me suck in my breath, and I saw the dogs lift their heads and look at me as if to say, "Give us five minutes more!" The moon cast a cold glow over the cabin, and the smoke from the stove gushed out of the chimney as though it couldn't get out fast enough.

Andrew had pointed out to everyone that the only way to have a successful patrol was to be on the trail before nine in the morning and stop at about four in the afternoon so that camp could be made in the daylight and our hard-working dogs would get enough rest. So on this morning our sleds were packed, the dogs were harnessed and we left the cabin at 8:55.

The moon shone brightly until just before 10:00, and the sun rose over the hills twenty minutes later. At first the dogs went very well in spite of the bitterly cold weather, which was made worse by the south wind that we had to face, and in spite of the beauty that surrounded us, my mind concentrated entirely on keeping warm. I tried keeping my face averted, and whenever I could let go of the sled, I tried covering my face with my big mitts, but it didn't seem to help and my nose began to freeze. I had been unable to find my scarf when I was packing up in the dark, so as we continued travelling into the wind, I had to keep rubbing my nose with my gloved hand to prevent frostbite. It was one of those mornings when the cold seemed to penetrate every nook and cranny of my clothes, and I stood on the back of the toboggan trying to keep my clothes from touching me, hoping that some warm air would fill in the space between skin and undershirt. I took shallow breaths as though that would prevent my skin from touching my freezing cold clothes, then the cold would force me to jump off the back of the toboggan and jog for a while. But when I breathed in deeply, my nostrils

Bill Antaya's frosty face reflects the effects of travelling into an icy wind.

seemed to freeze together, and when I exhaled, ice immediately formed and my beard was soon frozen to my collar. My hands felt cold all day, and if I had to handle the dog harnesses at all, it was quite painful and any heat I had managed to accumulate was soon lost.

The dog teams were all steaming in the frigid air, and in the red morning sunlight it looked as though they were glowing. It was too cold for me to try to take any photographs, and in any case, all my cameras were frozen solid even though they were wrapped inside my sleeping bag. A camera that Dave Sullivan had lent me had frozen with the lens shutter open.

We passed Sucker Creek and came to Three Cabin Creek where there was another cabin, but we didn't stop. When we did finally stop for lunch, I had some dry fish, bannock and a bar of chocolate. This

With its big wood stoves the cabin provided luxurious accommodation where Bill Antaya and Abe Koe could relax for awhile.

along with a couple of mugs of tea soon had me feeling fit for the trail again. However, all afternoon the dogs seemed to be tired out, and by the time we arrived at Road River, they were down to a walking pace. I was relieved to see that it wasn't only my team that was suffering; Bill Antaya was almost half an hour behind me.

The Gwich'in chief, John Tetlichi, and his wife were at their cabin at Road River, and they welcomed us into their home when we arrived in the late afternoon. We all managed to squeeze inside where it was lovely and warm. Chief John told us that it had been minus forty-five degrees Celsius that morning, though it had risen to minus forty by dusk.

That evening we tried fixing up the game warden's radio with an aerial fastened to a tree, but there was no reception except for static, so we decided not to carry it with us any longer. It was heavy and bulky, and if it had poor or no reception at this point, it was doubtful that it would improve as we got farther away. Even if the RCMP were to fly over us in the mountains, the radio would be frozen up and we wouldn't want to start putting up an aerial when the wind was blowing at minus fifty degrees anyway. Chief John said that he would return the radio to the game warden for us when he went back to Fort McPherson in the next day or two.

When we calculated our travel distance for that day, we realized that we had come forty-five kilometres, which helped to explain why our dogs were so tired. We ate a supper of pre-cooked beans, hamburger, bannock and coffee, and because we were socializing with the chief and his wife, we didn't get to bed until eleven. By that time I was physically tired, and the heat from the stove almost had me sleeping on my feet. I was very glad when the chief offered us sleeping room on his floor and we didn't have to go out into the cold.

# GOING VERY BAD ALL DAY

As Christmas Eve came to a close the RNWMP patrol passed Road River and made camp for the night on the Peel. In the morning they would enter Trail Creek, which was not much farther on.

Christmas day dawned, but unlike most other people in the country they did not relax and take life easy. This would be just another ordinary day on the trail for the policemen. They did their usual morning chores of cooking and eating breakfast, breaking camp and making preparations for another day of travelling in the dark. As usual the dogs were quite eager to be off and away.

At 10:15 they arrived at the mouth of Trail Creek and located the cache of dried fish that the constable had left for them some weeks earlier to help them on their way. The patrol stopped only long enough to load the bales of fish onto the toboggans. Travelling conditions improved greatly as soon as they entered this sheltered creek, quite a relief for them after facing the bitter cold wind on the Peel.

December is a cold month north of 60°, and when the sun sets over the southern horizon, the dusk that follows for the next month is fraught with freezing mists that cover the land, and the temperature remains very cold. Daylight comes at about eleven in the morning and dusk settles over the land again by the middle of the afternoon. For this reason, Inspector Fitzgerald made camp on Trail Creek at 2:15 that day to give his men and their dogs time to rest, but as they put up their tent the cold mists settled around them once again and the temperature dropped to minus thirty-five degrees Celsius. However, they were now twelve kilometres up the creek in a stand of timber that provided a good supply of dry spruce for the stove and small green spruce boughs for the floor of the tent.

The inspector then sent Constable Kinney and Special Constable Carter ahead up a small tributary stream to break trail to make the journey easier for them the next day. It was up this small creek that they met some First Nations people, and Fitzgerald was able to hire one of the men and his dog team to help break a trail across a 128-kilometre portage. He was paid three dollars per day for his trail-breaking efforts, and even though they only covered nineteen kilometres the next day, without his help they would not have got even that far. Fitzgerald noted in his diary: "Going very bad all day, had to break through almost a metre of snow and only made 19 kilometres. Climbed 243 metres."

By the time the men emerged from the creek the next day, they had climbed another 304 metres and the scenery before them was of valleys and mountain ranges stretching out forever. They were now in a very exposed location where the winds could be strong enough to blow a man over. It was here they were caught up by the other Aboriginals who had followed their trail, and they travelled together as far as Caribou Born Mountain where they all set up camp.

The next morning they parted with their Aboriginal companions except the man that they had hired and set out early to make the most of the daylight as they headed for the Caribou River. The snow conditions did not improve, and Fitzgerald reported travelling twenty-two kilometres one day and only fourteen kilometres the following day when the temperature plummeted to minus fifty degrees Celsius with a light wind.

On December 31 they reached another creek, and just before entering it, as they went over a knoll on the hillside, they caught a glimpse of the sun. It would have been a heartwarming sight for them as they fought the elements. The bitterly cold days had been hard on them and the continuous deep snow drained the reserves of their energy as they took turns breaking trail, but there on the last day of the year was the sun.

Their good spirits were lost the very next day. January 1, 1911, brought them a heavy snowstorm that lasted all day. They were only able to make one push forward, and after reaching a cabin seventeen kilometres up a creek, they called it a day and camped in the cabin. That night Fitzgerald paid off the trail breaker so that he could return to camp. He was paid for five days of breaking trail and three days for his return trip, which amounted to a total of twenty-four dollars for breaking trail through snow that averaged ninety-one centimetres deep.

# LUXURY BEHIND US

At 10:10 on the morning of February 18, 1970, we saw the sun just coming over the horizon, but as the temperature was minus forty-three degrees Celsius, it didn't do much to warm us physically. However, we all commented that it was nice to see it even if we couldn't feel it. At least there was no wind, which made a huge difference when we were moving forward.

After a breakfast of pancakes, beans and fried meat followed by coffee, the latter courtesy of Chief John Tetlichi, we set off on the trail again. We left the Peel River at this point and started to climb—and quite a climb it was, too. The dogs had to strain so much to get up that steep incline that when they leaned forward, their heads were almost into the snow. I would heave the sled a metre forward while yelling at them to go, and in this way we climbed bit by bit until we reached the top, exhausted but glad that this part was over. Then I sat on my sled to catch my breath and told the dogs that I was pleased with them, a comment that they seemed to appreciate as they looked at me and lazily wagged their tails. Of course, they could have been humouring me.

After that, we travelled on a series of small lakes with portages cut between them because this was John Tetlichi's trapline and the route that he took to get to the mountains when he was hunting. Then suddenly we came to an old seismic cutline—something that Fitzgerald could have done with, but in his time it did not exist. This cutline took us right to the foot of the Richardson Mountains, so we stopped for a lunch of dried fish mixed with cranberries and drank several mugs of tea. I had already discovered that drinking tea without milk was quite refreshing, though in the evening when Andrew made a pot of coffee, I really enjoyed the luxury of powdered cream in it with a table-spoonful of sugar.

By 2:30 that afternoon my dogs were tired out, and just when I was wondering how long it would be before we would halt for a tea break, we came across two Gwich'in hunters, Willie Firth and Jim Robert, who were just leaving their hunting camp. We stopped and made tea at their camp and I ate frozen bacon and pancakes. Bill Antaya was having an equally hard time with his dogs, which were tired out, but fortunately after the break we only went about two kilometres before we stopped to make preparations to camp for the night. There were lots of caribou, moose and marten tracks all around us, and William Vittrekwa thought that we should see some caribou "maybe to-morrow."

We tied the dogs up, making sure that they couldn't get at each other because they were tired and hungry and their patience with each other was down to zero. It would only take one inquisitive dog straying within his neighbour's territory for the hair to fly. Then these "poor, tired" dogs would launch into a winner-take-all fight, and if they were not separated, one of them could end up dead.

We had been fortunate in staying in cabins up to this point on the trip, but now those luxuries were behind us. This was the first night that we slept in tents. We had three canvas tents with us, one of which was a bit smaller, so when we were discussing who would go where, the men said that the "three leaders" should share the smaller tent, Bill Antaya would share with George Robert, Abe Vaneltsi and Jim Vittrekwa, and the rest would sleep in the other tent. That meant that

Andrew Kunnizzi, William Vittrekwa and I would be in the small tent, and we set out to get it ready.

Seeing all those men prepare camp was a sight to behold. No one really gave any orders, they just set to and did what had to be done. Cutting poles for the tents, about nine or ten per tent, then cutting dry wood into stove-length pieces, green boughs for the tent floors, wood for a fire outside to cook the dog food on, men going backwards and forwards on snowshoes, tramping down the snow to make a firm foundation for the tents—it seemed like a myriad of things all going on at once. I must have looked like the dopey white man as I took this in, and all I was thinking was that these guys kept calling me their patrol leader. Finally Andrew told me that my job was to flatten a space out for our tent with my snowshoes and I was glad to be doing something useful. Besides, it was hard to go wrong tramping down snow.

A trapper's canvas wall tent was surprisingly warm at minus forty. A carpet of spruce boughs insulated the floor from the snow and permafrost.

In the evenings Andrew Kunnizzi would melt a pail of snow water to make a pot of coffee, which he enjoyed with a cigar.

The tents were all the same style, trapper's tents made of medium-weight white canvas with a hole at the door end for the stovepipe to go through. Most other Indian or commercial tents had the stovepipe going out through the roof, but this was the style preferred by the Gwich'in as in a heavy snowstorm the snow would not get into the stove and put the fire out. They set their tents within a surrounding berm of snow, the snow being tramped down in the centre where the tent would actually be set so that there was a lot of head room inside.

When some of the young men brought over the cut poles, I helped—at least I think I helped—to put the tent up. We stood two crossed poles outside at either end of the tent and balanced a ridge pole on them before pushing several two-metre poles into the snow on either side of the tent to secure it. As Andrew and William kept bringing spruce boughs and throwing them just inside the tent, I knew that my next job was to place them on the floor of the tent for insulation. It was William Vittrekwa's wife, Mary, who had shown me how to do this years earlier when I stayed with them in their caribou hunting camp at Rock River in the Richardson Mountains. Now I laid the branches on the floor with the cut end pushed down so that there were no sharp pieces to poke us unexpectedly in some soft place in our anatomies. For the tent door we fastened a thin quilt over that end of the tent so that it hung down outside and touched the ground. Whenever anyone came in or out, this "door" was scooped aside; then it fell neatly back into place, effectively closing the door.

Finally, when the floor was ready, Andrew put the metal stove and chimney together, this stove being one he had manufactured with his sheet metal bending equipment at home. He placed the stove on a pair of green logs near the door of the tent, and within moments he had a fire crackling in it. Very soon we could feel some heat and the sweet smell of warm spruce boughs began to permeate everything. I brought in a large pot of clean snow to put on the stove so that by the time we had our personal things organized there would be water for tea—as long as we kept filling the pot up with snow. Meanwhile, we unloaded the sleds and brought our things inside. It was difficult to leave the warm tent to go outside and make the dogs' supper, but it was something that could not be left undone after all their hard work, and it had to be done as soon as possible for their sake.

It seems to be understood, in camping, that the first time the tent is pitched each person chooses a spot in it for himself, and that spot remains his for the entire trip. I had noticed that on all my camping forays I chose the far left corner of the tent, and if by some accident someone else joined us and took that place, it annoyed me.

We enjoyed a supper of caribou meat and soup followed by coffee and tea, and then Andrew surprised me as we were lying there relaxing by bringing out a cigar and puffing on it like a professional.

"Andrew, I didn't know that you smoked!" I said with what must have been surprise in my voice.

"Ah, this is something that I learned to like after a hard day's work when I lived in Dawson. This and a good cup of coffee!" He laughed and then started reminiscing about the days when he had lived in Dawson and some of the trips he had made. Once he had travelled from Fort McPherson via the Wind River all the way to Mayo to pick up his widowed sister and bring her back with him. William Vittrekwa joined in and talked about some of the people that he and Andrew had both known in their Dawson days. I marvelled that although we had travelled thirty-seven kilometres that day and were all tired, old Andrew and William seemed as fresh as the day we set off, and they had carried out their chores as if they had been on holiday.

The night was beautiful and clear and the stars twinkled in the blue-black sky, and as the full moon came into view over the trees, it made me feel that we could travel anywhere by its light. Later, as I lay in my sleeping bag listening to the fire crackling in the stove and smelling the aroma of the spruce boughs under me, I was startled when all sixty-seven dogs started howling, certainly not in unison but with great dramatic effect. Then the howling ceased abruptly as though the conductor had dropped his baton, and the sheer pleasure of it made me smile. I have experienced this phenomenon many times over the years and it still enthralls me. How do the dogs know to stop on cue? What made them start in the first place? Was it some far-off wolf calling or some primeval urge to sing to the moon?

The following morning the temperature was minus thirty-five degrees Celsius, and everyone felt the cold right from the start. I was reluctant to crawl out of my warm sleeping bag, but as the tent warmed up, I pulled on my trail pants and got ready. Huddling around the stove, we made a quick breakfast of caribou meat, porridge oats and stewed apples. We ate, washed it down with a cup of coffee and broke camp in less than half an hour. At 10:30, after we had been on the trail for almost an hour, the sun showed pink against the mountains. William Teya, Abe Koe and Jim Vittrekwa took turns breaking trail with their snowshoes, and the going was quite tough. The person walking ahead was followed closely by a second man who helped to make the trail firmer for the sleds. The driverless dog teams followed, and if for some reason they got hung up or if a sled tipped, the person next in line behind them straightened things out so that the snowshoers could keep going. In spite of the cold, the walkers soon dropped their parkas by the side of the trail and the next person to go by picked them up and put them on top of his loaded sled, and then as soon as there was a changeover, the dropped parkas were immediately required. And so the day went on, kilometre after kilometre, the snowshoers rotating about every hour.

Sometime around noon when we stopped for lunch, we saw the RCMP plane fly overhead, circling so we knew that they had seen us. We waved but we were not sure if they could see it, the plane having to fly high because of the possibility of strong downdrafts in the mountains.

As we neared the summit of Vittrekwa Creek, a very cold wind sprang up. I was surprised to see that the temperature had actually risen to minus twenty-six degrees so I tried taking a few photographs with my now unfrozen cameras.

All that day the men continued to take it in turns breaking trail with only a few stops for a fire and a mug of tea. When William Vittrekwa said that we were getting close to Rock River, it was decided that we would make camp in a stand of spruce trees. The setting up of camp proceeded as usual, but while I was walking around the campsite on snowshoes in the deep snow, I suddenly had an acute pain in my knee, which got worse and worse, so that by the time the tent was set up, I could barely hobble around and was glad to be able to sit in the tent as it warmed up and put an elastic bandage around the affected knee. This helped somewhat and I was able to feed my dogs without having to ask someone else to do it—that would have made me feel like a real wimp. I would have felt really bad if I was hurt because I had told everyone I would be needed on this trip to be of help to others if they were hurt. I had never imagined that I might be my own first patient.

We blew out the candle in the tent at 11:00 p.m., having travelled twenty-four kilometres that day.

# LOST AND COLD

 After their trail breaker left them, the four men of Inspector Fitzgerald's patrol found that the difficulties of the trail continued unabated. They had to cut their way through brush and driftwood, which twice prevented them from following the creek, and by the time they reached the Wind River, the dogs were just about played out. Here the snow was soft and deep, and to add to their troubles, as Fitzgerald reported in his diary, the temperature had dropped to minus fifty-five degrees Celsius, and the slight headwind made the cold penetrate their normally warm clothing.

Frostbite afflicted some of the men but not enough to cause them concern, and when they came to open water on the Wind River, all thoughts of frostbite vanished as they sought a place to cross without getting themselves or their dogs wet. Water appears on top of the ice when either the ice cracks and the pressure of the water beneath it is forced upward or the ice freezes to the gravel at the bottom and water from tributary creeks or mountain springs runs out over it. The water could be either centimetres or metres deep and at times may not even have any ice beneath it at all, depending upon the drainage around the creek. It will often take days to freeze over, and meanwhile it will be hissing and cracking in the sub-zero temperatures. And to make matters worse, sometimes an ice fog will develop above it.

At last, after passing Mount Deception, they managed to reach the Little Wind River, but patches of open water still plagued them. They still had to avoid getting the dogs' feet wet in the intense cold because this could quickly cripple them and they would be unable to pull the sleds.

By January 10 the temperature had moderated to a mere minus twenty-eight degrees, but fortunately there had been enough cold weather before that to finally freeze the stretches of open water. However, the dogs now experienced some difficulty pulling the heavy sleds as they tried to get a grip with their claws on the smooth icy surface of the river. The men also had to tread carefully, testing the thickness of the ice as they went, as it would have been deadly if they or their dogs fell through it.

Now the weather improved daily, and apart from one day when they all got their feet wet in some overflow, the travelling was good. Normally Inspector Fitzgerald would have been happy with this turn of events, but something happened that took his mind off such mundane things as the weather. The men had stopped for a noon break, and he decided to send the guide, Special Constable Carter, on ahead to look for the portage that they should take. Three hours later Carter returned to report that he could not find it.

The patrol continued on up the river, but they soon found that it was getting very narrow, an indication that they must have travelled too far up it and missed the portage. They made camp and once again Carter was sent out, but when he again returned without recognizing the creek, the only conclusion they could reach was that they were definitely too far up the river. They retraced their steps for eight kilometres and came to a small creek that Carter thought was Forrest Creek, the one they should be following. They trekked up it for six kilometres before deciding that it was the wrong one, and so returned to the Little Wind River, which they went down for three kilometres before making camp. Once again Carter was sent out to find the creek, but when he returned to the camp, he was unsure if he had found it.

On January 14 all the men had to wait in camp because of a very strong gale that lasted all day. These strong mountain winds occur quite frequently without warning when the heavy cold air at higher elevations literally slides down the mountains to replace the warmer air in the valleys and mountain passes. But because of the day's rest, they were all set to go again the following day and were on the trail by 7:30. They soon came to the east branch of the Little Wind River, and by 3:15 p.m. they were camping at, as Fitzgerald wrote, "what is supposed to be Forrest Creek."

On January 16 they went almost ten kilometres up the creek before finding that it was not Forrest Creek, so they had to retrace their steps. That afternoon Fitzgerald sent Carter out once again, but he had no success in finding the right creek. Fitzgerald knew that it was no use all of them going up and down the creeks, so early the next morning he sent Carter and Constable Kinney out to investigate a river that ran south-southeast, but after following it all day, they returned to report that it went straight up into the mountains. Carter was convinced that it was not the right one.

While Carter and Kinney were investigating their assigned river, Inspector Fitzgerald went off on his own to follow a river that ran toward the south, but he could not find any tree or bush cuttings that would indicate that other people had travelled that route. When he completed his diary that night he noted, "Carter is completely lost and does not know one river from another." To add to his growing concern, the worried patrol leader added:

We have now only ten pounds [4.5 kilograms] of flour and eight pounds [3.5 kilograms] of bacon and some dried fish. My last hope is gone and the only thing I can do is to return, and kill some of the dogs to feed the others and ourselves unless we can meet with some Indians. We have now been a week looking for a river to take us over the Divide, but there are dozens of rivers and I am at a loss. I should not have taken Carter's word that he knew the way from the Little Wind River.

They broke camp to return to the Peel River at 7:45 on the morning of January 18, and now that they were following a good trail, they managed to travel thirty-two kilometres before making camp.

# CARIBOU STEW AND BEANS

On Friday, February 20, our Dempster patrol started out early after eating a breakfast of bacon, caribou stew, bannock and jam. We were now facing a west wind, which as usual was a chinook wind, and although this made it a little warmer for travelling, the change was not too noticeable because it added a wind chill factor. There were some clouds in the sky and the wind was blowing snow off the mountains. The sun only showed itself briefly as its rays struck some distant mountain top.

We entered Rock River where the ice was a beautiful blue colour, but it was really slippery. Where the incline was downward, I rode my brake to prevent the sled from rear-ending the dogs, but where the ice had bulged, it caused the sled to fishtail, and I had a hard time preventing it from tipping over when it hit a protruding piece of ice or a chunk of driftwood. Standing on my claw brake at the rear of the sled resulted in an awful screeching noise, and soon ice pellets coated the back of my parka.

Lunch that day consisted of caribou meat and a doughnut. After travelling for thirty-two kilometres we made camp in a place that someone said was called Second Rock River. There was thick brush here and this proved providential as it snowed quite heavily during the night. During the day I had noticed that a number of the dogs' feet were bleeding because of the sharp pieces of ice that surrounded some of the patches of crusty snow they were running on, and as soon as we stopped for the night, they got busy licking their wounds. I examined each dog's feet, taking special notice of Silver's damaged foot. But apart from a few grazes every dog was in good condition, and although I had contemplated putting booties on them, I did not think that it was worth it, especially if all the dogs did was eat them minutes after I had struggled to put them on.

I placed good soft spruce boughs so that the dogs would have insulated beds where they were tied. Most of them seemed to appreciate this, but I had one dog, Nicki, a very likable ginger-coloured but rather stupid dog, who wouldn't know if he was bedded down on a pillow or an ice block. He worked hard all day and was quite affectionate, but all he knew was "go" and "stop." When he was ready to rest in the evening, he would do the usual three or four turns over the spruce branches and then plonk himself down beside them.

We took a tea break every two hours when the going was tough. Abe Koe and Fred Vittrekwa wait to get to the kettle on the fire.

The Richardson Mountains look down over the isolated patrol with nobody else around for hundreds of kilometres.

Supper that night was bacon and beans, bannock and coffee. I tried some caribou stomach, which the others seemed to relish, but my stomach didn't like the competition and I couldn't get any of it down. Afterwards Bill Antaya came around to our tent to visit for a while, and William and Andrew took it in turns to tell us tales of hunting at which they laughed uproariously. We turned in at 11:00, which was getting to be our usual "lights out" time, although by then I could hardly keep my eyes open.

It snowed quite heavily during the night and continued for most of the next day. We had been travelling down the Rock River and now had to climb out of the creek up a high bank where the snow was very deep and soft. However, once we got on top, the snow was firm and the travelling easy, except where the wind had scoured the snow away and the lumps and tufts of grass, so common on the tundra, made the trail rather lumpy. When we stopped to eat lunch, to everyone's surprise a herd of caribou crossed the creek behind us, and even though we only saw them for a matter of seconds, William Teya had his gun out and managed to shoot one. This was all the meat that we needed just then because we couldn't carry very much, but all the men were happy to have fresh supplies.

We came to a halt for the night at Snare Creek after travelling forty kilometres. As we made camp, the last rays of the sun shone on us, then after it had set, the moon came out and did its best to light up this arctic vista.

It was cooler that night, but we had a very relaxed evening. Most of the men played cards in the big tent, but some of the men joined us to discuss the route, and they kept the stove roaring so that it was almost too hot in there. William Vittrekwa was in his element with an audience and started telling stories of hunting and trapping in the area we were travelling through. Even though he spoke in the Gwich'in language, he used his hands to describe the mountains and creeks, the hunting and shooting. I couldn't understand everything he said, but with his gestures I soon had a pretty clear picture in my mind of what he was saying. Bill Antaya and I just sat and listened, absorbed by his gesticulations and toothless laughter.

That night I noted in my diary that "this place feels like the middle of nowhere!" But in fact, it reminded me of upper Stoney Creek, close to Fort McPherson, where I had camped with my family several times over the years. Once you get into the mountains, everywhere you look is barren, icy and cold with only a few small trees along the creeks and far below in the valleys. But on a clear day you can see for miles in the crystal-clear air.

Although Abe Koe had told me that they didn't need a map and I had agreed with him that the old men could find their way without one, I wasn't so sure about some of the young men. Each evening Andrew, William and George would tell the younger men who would be out in front breaking trail the next day what they should be looking for, where the mountains were and if there was any danger from creeks that were notorious for having open water on them. I would then pull out my map to plot our progress, and immediately Abe would want to know exactly where we were and which direction we were going and how far we had come. Then he would take over the map and study it carefully.

On Monday, February 23, we had quite an easy day. We breakfasted on leftover soup, bannock, bacon and porridge (in that order!) and left camp at 8:45. After travelling only eleven kilometres, we came to Crumbles Lake, so-called because someone had once left some commercial dog feed there. And now here we were so many years later arriving at our first cache of dog food that Great Northern Airways had brought for us. The lake was at quite a high elevation with only some small birch and scrub willows surrounding it, and the snow had been packed hard here by the wind, but the plane's ski marks were still visible in the snow, and out in the middle of the lake stood the forty-five-gallon drums of dog food, which not even the voracious ravens had been able to get into. We used an axe handle to pry open the drum lids, filled our sleds with the feed, then stopped for a bit to have some lunch while William Teya and Fred Vittrekwa went moose hunting. Afterwards, we took the feed a short distance farther and made a very early camp. I was quite excited because Muriel had managed to send a letter north and it had been put into one of the barrels, so I caught up on news from home. Having the letter made me feel even farther away

Abe Koe using my binoculars to check for signs of caribou or moose.

from my family, but it was good to know that I was in their thoughts and that they were okay way down south.

The two hunters returned without seeing any game, so once the camp was made and the dogs fed, we had an early supper of caribou meat, soup, bannock and jam. Afterwards, some of us did some minor repairs to our sleds and harnesses and visited back and forth between the tents. I tried to fix a small transistor radio that had broken when it was frozen and brittle. Suddenly during a lull in the conversation the radio came on loudly with a program from the BBC in London, England; then, just as suddenly, it faded away and I couldn't coax another sound from it. I returned to my tent, wrote up my diary and marked my map with where I thought we were. On my last visit outside I looked up into the clear dark sky and the heavens seemed crowded with twinkling

The sled dogs had to be fed by their owners to prevent any accidents from occurring from some of the more vicious dogs.

stars. The Great Bear looked so clear I thought it would growl. I had never seen it so perfectly defined before.

The temperature was about minus twenty-four degrees Celsius, and as Andrew snuggled down in his sleeping robe, he mentioned that even though we had only come eleven kilometres that day, he thought we were making good time so far. To me this information was comforting as it was coming from someone who had trod these trails before.

The next morning just as we were leaving camp, my metal dog pot, which was fastened on the front of my load, hit a tree, tearing in two. There was no point in keeping it, so I left it behind. I would have to share someone else's pot in order to feed my dogs.

We spent a pleasant day travelling down the Eagle River, although there were some difficult portages for us to negotiate, and the deeper snow on these portages made the dogs work hard as the sleds were heavier, having been restocked with dog feed and the shared caribou. I took a turn breaking trail on snowshoes and got absolutely lathered walking behind Jim Vittrekwa, who set a fast pace. I managed to keep up for about an hour and a half, then gave way to one of the others who was a lot more fit than I was. I was soaked with sweat and had to change my shirt and thermal vest, and even that was quite an experience, stripping off with a breeze blowing into my armpits at minus twenty. I tucked my sweaty shirt underneath one of the sled ropes where it soon froze solid.

We noticed that as we travelled southwards there was a lot more daylight in both the morning and the evening, and this was especially appreciated first thing in the morning when we were getting ready to hit the trail. That evening, just as we were pulling into a stand of trees

Opposite: Two men on snowshoes would go ahead of the dog teams to break trail. William Teya and Fred Vittrekwa take their turn.

to make camp, a yellow plane flew over and circled half a dozen times. A couple of the young men rushed into the nearest open area and, racing around as best they could without snowshoes on, they wrote "OK" in the metre-and-a half depth of snow, which was quite a feat. We wondered if the people in the plane were planning to drop a message to us, but unless it had been really well marked, we wouldn't have been able to locate it. We saw that there was lots of open water on the river near our campsite because the high canyon walls at this point leave it few places to go when there is overflow. We expected that we would have to make a lot of portages to get around it the next day.

Peter Nerysoo was quite excited and kept looking around for signs of old camps, and then I remembered Andrew telling me that Peter had lived in this area with his parents when he was very young. However, it didn't look as though he recognized anything in particular. I found it quite enthralling to think that less than fifty years ago people had lived and thrived in these isolated places, even though just surviving would have been a challenge. It must have been especially difficult raising young children out here. While we were just "passing through," Peter's family had stayed for weeks if not months hunting and trapping, and they had not carried a large supply of store goods with them.

For supper that night we dined on caribou backstrap meat along with tomato soup and then as usual we drank coffee and then lots of tea in the course of the evening. We had travelled twenty-four kilometres that day without too much difficulty and I wondered if the rest of the trip was going to be as easy—that term being relative, of course.

I woke the following morning feeling strangely warm. No frost on my beard or around my sleeping bag. I went outside and saw that there was a strong chinook wind blowing, and it had taken the temperature up to minus five degrees. What a change! Everything was wet and the snow was sticky and heavy. We packed up the tent, loaded the sleds and were all away by 9:00. We travelled a short way on the Eagle River, then turned off and started climbing higher. The wind blew stronger now, and the sky looked black toward the north and northwest. But in spite of this ominous weather, everyone seemed to be quite excited at the prospect of seeing the Blackstone Mountains, and as we travelled on, we did get a glimpse of them far to the south. The Blackstones were an indication that we were nearing the head of the Peel River at Eagle Plains. From here the Blackstone River flowed south toward the Klondike River and our destination.

I was surprised to see how many trees there were all around this plateau as I had gained the impression it was going to be quite desolate. We saw tracks of moose, caribou, marten and mink, and when we stopped for lunch, some of the men said that they were thinking of coming back this way and setting traps here. Others just said that they may come trapping here "one of these years." I thought it sounded just like people down south who go window-shopping and make a wish list.

While we were eating the usual bannock and beans and drinking tea, Andrew asked me if I would like to have a chunk of his cheddar cheese. As he cut off a generous portion for me, he said with a twinkle in his eye that he didn't think we were about to starve so he had broken into his survival rations. To help lighten my own load, I mixed two jars of powdered coffee cream in with my small canvas sack of sugar and dispensed with the two glass jars the cream had come in.

That day we came again to an old seismic road, which we were able to follow west over some rolling hills for a short distance. Around 4:30, when we came to a high point on the trail, we stopped to make camp. After days of no pain, my knee started acting up again, probably because I had spent some time breaking trail. I think that I had torn a semi-lunar cartilage, and it had chosen this inconvenient time to flare up again.

Later in the evening Abe Koe, one of our best trail breakers, came to me after cutting his foot with his axe. I could see that the cut needed some stitches because it was located where his snowshoe harness would rub against it. Abe was a tough guy but the thought of having stitches did not appeal to him at all. However, as we were talking about it, William Teya visited our tent to discuss the route that we would be taking the next day, so Abe did not make too much of a fuss in front of him or those two stalwarts Andrew Kunnizzi and William Vittrekwa, who sat there not saying anything, just looking. I froze the area on Abe's foot with the anaesthetic in my carefully protected first-aid kit and then after a few moments put in a few stitches. While I did

Taking advantage of the last few trees, which would give us kindling for a fire, we stopped for a tea break before going over the mountain.

this, William Vittrekwa told us how in the old days they had used tea or carbolic soap as a dressing for small wounds and how they would lay a beaver hair in a cut so that it would heal without a scar. I wasn't about to experiment with beaver hair so I applied some antiseptic and a dressing to Abe's wound. He seemed quite proud of the result, and when other men came into the tent, he had to tell them about his big wound that had needed "lots of stitches."

William Vittrekwa was very vocal every evening with his tales of trapping and hunting, while Andrew Kunnizzi was full of other kinds of information, and that night he laughingly told me the Gwich'in version of how a man came to be on the moon, a story that I neglected to write down. Andrew was usually more talkative in the mornings, and as we waited for the kettle to boil, he told me what it had been like to live in Dawson and the Yukon when he was a young man. He was an intelligent man and always curious, and he had spent hours watching people manufacturing items that were going to be used by the gold miners and asking questions, and so had learned something about blacksmithing, among other things. He hadn't written any of this down but made mental notes of things that interested him, and years later when he was living in Fort McPherson he began working with metal, always working from his remarkable memory. He had made dozens of camp stoves for the Gwich'in and had also constructed a working fish wheel, which proved quite effective in the strong Peel River current.

That night everything in the camp was wet through because of the chinook, and I sat on a caribou skin in my shorts while I wrote my diary, then went to bed about 10:30. The total distance travelled that day was twenty-four kilometres.

Near the summit at
Eagle Plains we had
to rest the dogs while
our guides gave us
fresh directions.

Each day of travelling was quite different and Thursday, February 26, was one of the most frustrating days for us. We saw some caribou, but the dogs starting barking and the caribou ran off, which was annoying because we were on the last of our meat. Next, the dogs belonging to the snowshoers who were breaking trail were so vicious that, when we approached to move them along behind their owners, they just growled and snapped at anyone who came near. They refused to move until the owners, realizing what was happening, whistled for them to follow.

The country that we were now going through was very brushy with low-lying willows that sprang back into our faces if we weren't constantly watching the person ahead. William Teya broke the head of his toboggan and had to stop for a while to cut a piece of birch so that he could fix it. We came across what looked like a small airstrip in the middle of nowhere and decided that it must have been created to bring in supplies for the seismic crew. On my map the strip simply had the name "Blacky" printed on it. The mountains began to look quite close and we were rewarded with a beautiful sunset, although we were all soaked through from the wet snow. The temperature stayed warm, about minus five degrees Celsius and we had travelled nineteen kilometres.

Sometimes I wondered just how much our patrol was like that of Inspector Fitzgerald because at times there seemed to be a few parallels, but on Friday, February 27, we had our own unique problem. It had started the night before when the men had come to our tent, a nightly occurrence during which Andrew would outline the characteristics of the land ahead of us. He would tell us what mountains we would see and which creeks to follow, and this would be interspersed with anecdotes about his life in this area with his parents.

On the Friday morning when we left camp, I was fourth in line behind William Teya, George Robert and Peter Nerysoo, and these three decided to take a shortcut up a road that varied from the plan that had been decided on the night before, but they said that they were following some caribou tracks. They continued farther east, then cut south on the next ridge. When we stopped to have lunch, most of the others caught up to us, but Abe Vaneltsi reported that Bill Antaya, Andrew and William had started up another of the old seismic roads, so now we became confident we would meet them at the summit.

After lunch when we stopped for a moment and looked to the south, we could see the headwaters of the Peel River as well as the mouth of the Blackstone where it seemed to slice down through the mountains. It was a beautiful but desolate panoramic view, just the deep valley between us and the Blackstone Mountains. There were no distracting noises, just the wind blowing over the hardened snow surface. It made me feel as though we were the only people in the world.

Knowing that we would all be heading for the Blackstone River, we started down the long, steep slope to the Peel far below us, following a really rough, brushy creek. It was the worst trail I had ever been on, and as I came toward the edge of the bank overlooking the river, my dogs just disappeared from sight right ahead of me. When I arrived at the brink moments later and saw the drop ahead that my dogs had disappeared over, I just let go of the sled and hoped that it wouldn't kill them when it hit them. Then I peered over the edge, and they were all standing on the ice below me wagging their tails as though they were having the time of their lives. I jumped down and moved them and the sled out of the way as two more teams came hurtling over the bank.

As there was still no sign of Andrew, William and Bill, we moved across the river toward the mouth of the Blackstone and started to set up camp. We figured that the others must have gone down the next creek as it wasn't so rough, and they would be joining us before long. I fired two sets of two .303 shells but got no response. Some of the men went moose hunting as there were moose and caribou tracks all around us in the willows, and George said that the tracks were quite fresh. I moved into the tent belonging to George Robert, Abe Vaneltsi and Jim Vittrekwa, taking the place of Bill Antaya, who was no doubt taking my place with William and Andrew wherever they were camped. I took over my favourite corner on the left side at the back of the tent, but I couldn't help but be worried. I didn't like to see the patrol split up, and although I knew that each group was in good hands, I was a bit worried because if the others had to break trail very far, it could tire them out.

The hunters came back without seeing any moose, but they confirmed that there were fresh caribou tracks mixed in with the moose tracks. They had decided that it would be worth going out again in the morning. That evening it snowed a bit, but as it was only light fluffy flakes, I spent some time outside fixing a split in one of my toboggan boards. That day we had added another twenty-four kilometres to our log, and we were still making good time.

# ONLY DOG MEAT AND TEA

 Inspector Fitzgerald's men, unlike us, were not at all happy. For one thing, they hated turning back, and for another, they had to shoot the first dog to provide meat for the other dogs. Worse yet, the dogs would not eat the meat offered to them, and the men ended up giving the dogs some of their precious dried fish instead. That night the men ate a small piece of bannock and a little dried fish.

The overflow water that had plagued the patrol on their outward journey provided even more trouble on the return trip. The Little Wind River was covered with overflow and there was no way around it, and at times the men had to drive their dogs through ankle-deep water. That night they shot another dog.

On January 20 another gale kept the patrol in camp all day, and at times it took all their strength just to keep the tent from blowing away. They ate the last of their flour and bacon, and Inspector Fitzgerald wrote in his diary: "All we have now is some dried fish and tea." He did not mention whether they had tried to eat any of the dog meat yet.

But their problems had only begun. After fighting the bitter temperatures and high winds, they were now faced with a day of melting snow as the mercury suddenly shot up to minus sixteen degrees Celsius. Twenty-four hours later it was back down to minus fifty degrees with a southwest wind blowing. Special Constable Carter's fingers were badly frozen, and the day was so cold that they were forced to stay in camp again. Meanwhile, another dog had to be killed for its meat.

The next morning they discovered that the Big Wind River had opened up right across, and Constable Taylor somehow found himself in water up to his waist while Special Constable Carter fell in up to his hips. They had to make camp immediately; otherwise, with the mercury hovering around minus forty-five degrees, the two men would have died of exposure within a very short time. It was 11:00 a.m. when they made camp, and before long both men were sitting in comparative comfort by the hot stove as their clothes dried out.

The inspector killed another dog and reported, "All hands made a good meal on dog meat."

By January 25 the patrol was slowly passing Mount Deception again and though they could see parts of their old trail, the men were weary and hungry. By this time the remaining dogs were in poor condition from lack of food and could barely pull the toboggans over the drifted-in trail. The men were existing on nothing but dog meat and tea, and even the smallest chore sapped their strength. It took them three hours to find their way around some open water, and Fitzgerald now acknowledged in his diary that the men and dogs were getting weak.

They reached one of their old camps at a place called Waugh's Creek after prospector Harry Waugh, who had left this area when he heard that gold had been found on Bonanza Creek near to Dawson City. The men searched around to see if there were any scraps of food left there but could find nothing, so they had to kill another dog. They now had just nine dogs left.

Perhaps from eating dog meat, especially the liver, which is very high in vitamin A and as a result very toxic to humans, Constable Taylor became ill the next day, and the going was really tough on the others. Their outgoing trail was now blown over and fresh snow was falling again. They camped that night at a cabin on Mountain Creek and cached one sled and wrapper after killing another dog. They also left seven single dog harnesses, which they no longer required.

The next day all the men reported feeling sick, and Fitzgerald decided it was caused by eating dog livers. A few days later Inspector Fitzgerald wrote in his diary that the men's skin was peeling from their faces and other parts of their bodies, and their lips were swollen and split. He again blamed the eating of dog meat for this malady.

On the first day of February they started the trek around Caribou Born Mountain following their old trail. They were all feeling the cold, and even though the temperature rose from minus forty-three degrees Celsius to minus thirty-five degrees, it didn't make them feel any better. However, they managed to travel almost twenty-six kilometres before making camp. There they shot yet another dog for food.

# INGENUITY SAVES THE DAY

Our patrol was still separated, most of us on the Peel River, the other three somewhere on the headwaters where the Blackstone and Peel meet, so William Teya and Fred Vittrekwa walked up the river to the next creek to see if they had come that way. While they didn't see any sign of them, they did spot a beaver, but they were so surprised that they didn't get it. It went into a hole in the riverbank and they decided

William Teya and Peter Nerysoo help cut up a moose that George Robert had shot at the mouth of the Blackstone River. Peter scooped up the blood into a bucket to mix with his dog feed.

to wait for it to come out again, but it was too wise and stayed hidden. Meanwhile, we dismantled our tent and moved over a portage to the Blackstone River. I wanted to be camped in a place where either we would see them or they would see our camp, because they had to come down the Blackstone to go south. And even if we didn't see them, the dogs would certainly alert us to anyone in the vicinity. We made tea at 3:15 and I asked Fred Vittrekwa to walk up by the Peel River and up a hill where he might catch a glimpse of them. William Teya and Jim Vittrekwa went hunting, but William came back after seeing only fresh moose sign and Jim came back after seeing nothing at all.

About 4:30 p.m. Fred appeared with William Vittrekwa, Andrew Kunnizzi and Bill Antaya in tow. It was good to see them again, and though they were tired, they were otherwise okay. After leaving us they had headed for the ridge where we should have met them, but it had been heavy going so they camped for the night on the ridge. That morning they had come down the creek and were crossing the Peel when Fred had met them. I guess they were very glad to see him and have his help locating us. Of course, we had to tease each other about which group constituted the Lost Patrol.

By this time the day seemed to be warming up and the sun felt positively hot. As soon as camp was set with all of us together again, another four men went hunting, as we were very low on meat; I had eaten my last piece of caribou meat at breakfast. Just as it was getting dark three of the men came back empty-handed, but at 9:30 George Robert came back by the light of the moon, looking quite tired but happy because he had shot a cow moose about three kilometres away. Everyone else was very happy about this, too, and I was quite relieved that not only were we all together again but we also had a supply of meat waiting for us to pick up in the morning.

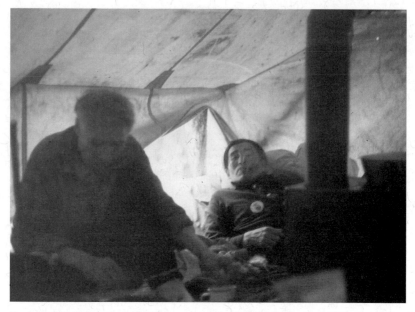

During a chinook we had a day of rest and feasting. George Robert and Peter Nerysoo make do with some northern air conditioning.

Andrew and William soon recovered from their exertions of the previous day and during the evening managed to tell us a few stories— all trapping and hunting stories, of course. One was about how one man went hunting caribou and the others drove the animals toward him. (I'm sure that the "him" was William himself!) When the caribou were really close, he found that his gun was frozen, so what did he do? Just what any thoughtful man would do when he has a frozen gun and is hungry for meat. He urinated on the rifle, thawing it out in time to get enough caribou to save the day.

This day we had only travelled eight kilometres but it was a very worthwhile eight kilometres.

March 1 was a day of relaxation and we just did what we wanted and took our time doing it. Andrew Kunnizzi, being a lay preacher in the Anglican Church, gathered some of the men together for a short Gwich'in church service. I visited Bill in his tent and chose to do some Bible reading on my own while Bill had a snooze. In the afternoon George Robert headed for his moose kill with a couple of the others to cut up the moose, so I rode down with them, sitting in George's empty carriole and carrying my snowshoes with me. The temperature had really climbed and everything was dripping wet. I checked my thermometer and saw that it was nearly five degrees above zero. This really was a chinook! It was just as well that we had taken the day off because it would have been a miserable day to travel and very tough on the dogs.

I took some photographs of the four men skinning the moose and cutting it up, then started to walk back, making a detour to an old shack that the men had seen when they were hunting. I think it was something left from the seismic survey, and I found some nails in it that Bill wanted so he could make repairs to his sled's lazyback. I then walked in a roundabout way to the camp to see if there was another moose in the vicinity, but just like the others, all I saw were tracks. By the time I got back, there was a cold north wind blowing and it had started to snow.

Abe Koe, Abe Vaneltsi and Fred Vittrekwa had left camp around 1:00 p.m. to break trail for the next day, and they didn't get back until 7:00 that evening. Supper consisted of fresh moose steaks fried in butter and hotcakes with bacon. I had thought of writing some letters, but for some reason my eyes became very heavy shortly after supper. I would have slept right through the night, but a few loose dogs made the others bark with jealousy and my sleep was interrupted a lot. I

We always made good fires to thaw out our fingers while the kettle was boiling.

didn't get up to see which dogs were loose, just hoping that they were not mine.

I woke at 6:15 the next morning feeling very cold, so I got up and made a good fire—something that I rarely did because William Vittrekwa was usually up first and made the fire and put a pot full of snow on the stove so that we could have tea. While I was getting things ready, I put on my down parka because the tent took quite some time to warm up. The wind was blowing strongly and I knew that today was going to be a tough one. I had been told that after a warm chinook wind the temperature could be guaranteed to plummet, and I had experienced this phenomenon several times before when camping in the Richardson Mountains. I was thankful that we had been able to get to the moose and butcher it before this cold weather hit us. A glance at the thermometer outside showed that the mercury was down to minus fifty-two degrees Celsius, so the wind chill factor would have been off the scale. According to the "Equivalent Wind-Chill Temperature Chart" that I carried, at minus fifty-two degrees Celsius with a wind of thirty miles per hour (forty-eight kilometres per hour) the wind chill temperature would be minus ninety-five degrees Celsius, at which temperature flesh will freeze in thirty seconds.

Of course, after we had relaxed in that balmy weather, the cold temperatures and wind felt doubly cold to all of us. But after breakfast we reluctantly packed everything up, leaving the stove until last, emptying the ashes out and setting it aside for about three minutes to cool down so it could be lashed to the sled. As the dogs were being harnessed up and the men had to fasten the clips with their bare hands, they grumbled that their hands were freezing. My own were almost numb, and by the time I was finished I could not feel my fingers. It was like trying to tie a knot with wooden fingers. Then later as they thawed out, they felt as though they were on fire.

In spite of the frigid temperatures, mineral "hot" springs on some creeks created stretches of open water, which could be quite perilous.

We left the campsite at 9:15, and the dogs worked well after their day of rest and a feed of fresh meat. In fact, they worked too well and we found ourselves travelling "bumper to bumper" down the river ice, and we could not get off and run behind our sleds to warm up.

At noon we made tea and ate fried moose meat, bacon and bannock. I gave Bill Antaya some of my stash of barley sugar because he was craving something sweet, a weakness that I had, too. I only had one candy bar left out of the twelve I had started with and three and a half boxes of barley sugar out of the seven at the beginning of the trip. The hot tea was a blessing both inside us and in our cups, as it almost managed to warm our hands. Andrew Kunnizzi told us that he expected we would be at Chappie (Chapman) Lake with another two good days of travel, but it looked farther than that on my map when I checked it out that evening. We continued down the Blackstone River all that day, passing quite a few areas of open water, which Andrew explained were from the hot springs in this area, but the water felt very cold when I put my hand in it for one brief moment.

There were numerous signs of both moose and caribou, and in one area we saw where wolves had brought down a moose and the snow was all trampled and bloody. There wasn't a moose bone left and only a smattering of its hair. Those wolves must have been hungry. I had seen evidence of wolf kills in another area, and there it had been plain that the wolves had stalked a moose that was browsing on some bushes. They had circled the animal and then by the look of the tracks in the snow they had come at their prey from every angle. One wolf had bitten into the moose's jugular, and blood had sprayed around as if it had come from a broken hose pipe. In spite of this, the moose had walked—or most likely staggered with wolves all over it—about twenty metres before it had finally fallen, and the wolves had virtually demolished it. Nature is not always pretty.

The mountains were awesome that day, the sun shining on the tops and the shadows making such a contrast between the rock and snow bluffs. There were few cornices that I could see; perhaps the winds just blew the snow completely away. I tried taking photographs with my half-frozen cameras, but the light meter that I used was not functioning for the same reason.

We travelled forty kilometres before making camp. When we were all relaxing in the tent after supper, I noticed for the first time how much the young men spoke in their own language. They were all fluent in English, which they spoke even to one another when out on the trail, and back in the village they had seemed almost embarrassed to be heard speaking Gwich'in. But here they were in the majority, and since the older men were more comfortable describing things in Gwich'in, they talked and talked, and the young men had some good conversations with the older men. I felt that I could have learned the language if I was with them all the time and if they didn't speak to me in English.

We turned in early, expecting that it was going to be a cold night.

On Tuesday, March 3, I noted in my diary: "If it was cold yesterday, it was freezing this morning!" I had slept reasonably well but kept waking up when my beard froze to my sleeping bag, and when I turned over it felt as though my face was being ripped off. All the tents had their stoves going by 4:00 a.m. but it seemed that they couldn't throw the heat any farther than half a metre.

My glasses that day were a writeoff because of the frost, and when I broke trail for a time my beard and my face were covered in frost. The whole morning seemed a blur of freezing toes, nose and fingers, and at the end of the day as I sat in the tent, my finger ends almost felt bruised. The temperature dipped to minus fifty-three degrees Celsius and the chill from the south wind made it at least twenty degrees below that.

We stopped for lunch at 11:15, and while we were making the fire, the dogs all started to bark. Looking up, we saw six caribou crossing the river just ahead of us. Three of the men went after them, but the rest of us were too cold to bother, and the three soon came back without shooting any of them.

About 3:00 p.m. it seemed to warm up a bit in the brilliant sunshine, and it became necessary for us to wear sunglasses to prevent snow blindness, but for me it was a frustrating exercise because my glasses still kept freezing up, and when the metal frames touched my cheek, it felt just like a burn.

We went over and through quite a lot of overflow that afternoon, and I found this an eerie experience as I could hear the thin ice cracking underneath the sled, and we had no idea how deep the water was in the creek beneath it. I remembered Inspector Fitzgerald's diary entries in which he wrote of falling through the ice in frigid temperatures.

An RCMP plane flew over us in midafternoon, but it had to stay quite high because, according to my map, the mountains surrounding us were over 1,500 metres high. We took this opportunity to stop and make tea and have some roasted moose meat as our bodies needed something warm. As usual, by the time we had cut down trees and hauled them to the firepit, we had started to warm up, and after hanging over the fire while we roasted meat and tended our teakettles, we soon felt better.

We made camp at 4:15 p.m. in a rather poor place. The trees here were mostly black spruce, which seem to grow only in swampy or muskeg ground. They were covered in a greenish-black hairy material, which looked like rotten old man's beard, a tree lichen that is a favourite food of caribou. Bill Antaya came to our tent to visit for a short time, and I think that the cold must have affected us because as we discussed the cold day and how we had suffered, we both cracked up laughing.

Andrew said that some of the men did not have very much dog feed left and that George Robert, who said he had been this way "two or three times before," thought that it was not far to Chapman Lake, where our second cache of dog food should be. Mind you, George had said that Chapman Lake was "only" three days' travel away when we were at Crumbles Lake, so I think that over the years the territory had shrunk in his mind. Fortunately, I had heeded William and Andrew's advice and carried the same amount of dog feed they did, and I figured it was going to be enough to get me to the next cache, though I knew that we would have to share with the others if they ran out. When I checked the map, it seemed to me that we still had another eighty kilometres to go to Chapman Lake, and the going had been much tougher that day with the cold and so much deep snow. We had only travelled twenty-four kilometres.

# DESPERATE GOING

Inspector Fitzgerald wanted to keep his remaining dogs as long as possible, so they had been feeding them small amounts of dry fish because up to then they had refused to eat the dog meat. Most northern sled dogs eat fish almost exclusively, summer and winter, so perhaps these dogs could smell the dried fish for as long as it lasted. But the patrol had now travelled over three hundred kilometres on dog meat after the dried fish had run out, and there was nothing else to feed the dogs. The inspector remained confident that they would make it back to Fort McPherson, and in his diary for February 3 he wrote: "We still have 100 miles [160 kilometres] to go but I think that we will make it alright but will only have three or four dogs left."

However, with the small number of dogs left and their lack of food, the patrol was only making about twelve kilometres a day, and the cold weather was making them very miserable. On one occasion Inspector Fitzgerald broke through the ice, and by the time a fire was made to dry him out, one of his feet was found to be slightly frozen. Falling into the water when the temperature is in the minus fifties is an emergency at any time, but for these men it was the worst thing that could possibly happen. This event burned up their much-needed calories and delayed them on the trail.

That same night they killed another dog, leaving them with

only five dogs to carry four men and their meagre supplies. Inspector Fitzgerald reported that everyone was "breaking out on the body and skin peeling off."

With at least another 160 kilometres to go before they reached Fort McPherson, Fitzgerald must have realized that they were going to be tough kilometres. He would have calculated that his five dogs would provide them with food for just another ten days, and at a diminished distance travelled each day they might travel only eighty kilometres in that time. It was not a very bright prospect for these stalwart men of the RNWMP, but they battled on through the cold and the snow, getting weaker every day. They finally reached the Peel River but they were disappointed to find that there was no fresh trail for them to follow. At that time very few Native people travelled from the Divide Mountains to Fort McPherson because the Yukon beckoned to them with all its exciting goods from "outside" and the general buzz of a gold-mining city. By comparison Fort McPherson must have been a very dull place. Fishing in the Mackenzie Delta and trapping muskrat in the myriad lakes between Fort McPherson and Aklavik did not start for another ten or fifteen years after Fitzgerald's time.

Trudging along day after day with another fifty-six kilometres to go after the last dog was eaten, Inspector Fitzgerald had to make the difficult decision to leave the two constables, Kinney and Taylor, in a camp on the Peel River while he and Special Constable Carter tried to forge ahead for help. In any case, the two young men did not have the strength to continue, and they all realized that to attempt to do so would hold up the progress of the other two. As the tent and stove had been left on the side of the trail the day before to lighten the load, the men had to stay in an open camp. They made a fire and put a kettle on it, and dropped small pieces of moosehide into it to provide some nourishment. Then they lay in their sleeping bags resting.

# LONG DAY

On Wednesday, March 4, we dawdled as we got ready to travel, hoping that the temperature would rise a degree or two before we hit the trail, so it was almost 10:00 when we finally pulled away from camp. Fortunately, the wind was behind us. Travelling over the ice on the creek was easier than on the portages because there was only a little snow on top of the ice, just enough for the dogs to get a firm grip as they pulled

Crossing Wolverine Glacier against a constant strong wind was hard on dogs and drivers.

us along. We had to go through some water, but it wasn't as much as we had gone through previously.

We crossed the Hart River portage shortly after our lunch break at 12:30 and came out onto the alluvial plain at the foot of Wolverine Glacier, a plain that had been created by thousands of years of melting ice and flooding rivers. The real glacier was farther west from where we were crossing, and from what I have heard and read of crossing glaciers, I was not sorry to give it a miss. There was no protection from the wind as we crossed this great expanse of ice and snow, and when it veered around and blew right into our faces, I could feel myself shrinking into my parka to try to get some protection from it. The dogs didn't seem to notice the cold wind and headed right into it. Their biggest problem was trying to bite at the hard snow to get a drink as they trotted along.

When we came to a small stand of trees, we stopped and made tea, and I was surprised to see that it was already 4:30, the time that we normally stopped to make camp. Of course, we were now moving steadily south, and the sun stayed up longer, and later on we would be reminded that even our watches had to be changed to reflect Yukon time. I finished off a moose rib that William Vittrekwa had roasted for me the night before and ate two frozen bannock buns, which I found were quite all right as long as I kept looking for the raisins, which added a little taste and interest to the meal. Afterwards, we carried on for another hour before making camp. That evening we cooked some dried beans with tomato soup and onion flakes, and it smelled really good, but as it was for the following day, I couldn't eat any of it.

We had travelled a total of forty-eight kilometres, a good distance for the day. We were now 466 kilometres from Fort McPherson.

On Thursday, March 5, we had what I referred to as "the long day." It started out quite normally but by the end of the day any fears about us not making our destination had been removed.

We broke camp at 9:30 and found that, although it was just as cold as the day before, the wind was now behind us, the sort of wind that passed you instead of followed you, and we made excellent time going over overflow ice and ice bulges, which we referred to as "glaciers." We made a quick lunch in some scrub willow in the middle of which we found a dry spruce tree that gave us enough wood for a fire. Andrew told us that he thought we might be as little as nine or ten kilometres from where we should see the new cutting for the Dempster Highway. Periodically we thought we could hear the sound of truck engines, but the sleds made so much noise on the ice it was hard to say for sure. Still, we looked and listened with anticipation.

True to Andrew's prediction, after travelling another ten kilometres, the man at the head of the line called out that he had reached the road and was actually standing on it. Soon we all emerged from the creek onto a rough gravel road that wound along beside the creek. Here we stopped for a time and congratulated one another, and I took a few photographs with the only camera that wasn't frozen up. At that point we heard a truck engine in the distance, but realizing that it was getting closer, we moved our dogs to the side of the road. It would have been terrible to have them come this far only to be run over.

It was quite funny to see the look on the truck driver's face when he came around the bend in the road and saw us standing there. He pulled over and we moved our teams on down the road past him. He didn't say a word, just stared at us with his mouth open. I came up to his cab and woke him from his reverie by asking him where he was going, and I was surprised that he didn't ask me the same question. He told me that he was hauling fuel oil to a road-building crew somewhere up the Dempster Highway. I asked him where Chapman Lake was, and he disappointed me by saying it was another sixteen kilometres down the road. I thanked him and called my dogs back to the business at hand. As we set off again, the truck remained there for quite some time, perhaps while the driver told people on his road radio frequency about the incredible sight he had just witnessed. I sincerely hoped he would tell other drivers of our presence so that they would slow down before reaching us.

Those sixteen kilometres to Chapman Lake seemed to go on forever. After winding our way around trees and over barren landscapes, travelling down a road was relatively boring in spite of the fact that we

With some relief we reached the fledgling Dempster Highway, which was under construction.

The beauty of the Yukon enthralled us all. To the dogs it was just the same old thing.

# THE LAST PATROL

Travelling down the Dempster Highway could have been monotonous if it wasn't for the grandeur of the mountains.

were passing through some of the most picturesque country in Canada. Where there were no trees to offer protection, the road seemed to funnel the wind between the mountains, and sometimes it threatened to blow us right off the road. Bits of shaley rock blew into our faces as the wind whirled around us. Around four we stopped on the side of the road where there was some protection from a stand of small spruce trees, made some tea and gave the dogs a chance to rest. The gravel on the road was making the sleds grind along, and I thought that the oak boards were going to be planed away before we got to Dawson. Here the sun beamed down on us, but the heat from it was lost in the cold wind.

It was 6:30 when we reached Chapman Lake and found our cache of dog food in its forty-five-gallon barrels sitting in the middle of the frozen lake. The barrels had been flown to Dawson City airport on a scheduled flight and then hauled by truck to the lake. We pulled

We camped in the only stand of trees left by the stampeders at Black City.

146

enough food out of the barrels for that night and, leaving the rest secured once more, we crossed the lake and stopped in a lonely stand of spruce about two kilometres away. These trees were a different variety from what we were used to as their needles were softer than the sharp needles of the spruce that we usually slept on, but they smelled just the same.

We had travelled a total of forty-eight kilometres since breakfast and were very tired. We put the tents up quickly, but it was very difficult in the high wind, and as there was not much snow to pack around them, we worried that if the wind got under them, they might just take off like great big balloons. By now the weather had turned quite warm and we were soon walking around without parkas on for the first time in weeks. The dogs sprawled where they were tethered, trying to find enough snow to roll in to cool themselves off.

Along the way we had passed a place that Andrew said was called "Calico Town," but you couldn't tell that there had ever been anything like a town there at all. There was a hunting camp at the location now, but Andrew explained that in the Klondike gold rush times the Gwich'in had established a tent village there, and the site had probably been used even before that when the people still travelled in their nomadic style in the mountains as they hunted caribou and moose. I recalled that Walter Alexie, a man I knew from Fort McPherson, had told me that he had been born in Calico Town and that the Trondek Hwech'in, the First Nation from the Moosehide village near Dawson City, also had connections to it.

The place where we camped also had a history. It had been known as "Black City," possibly getting the name from the Blackstone River. Once it had been thickly forested with spruce and pine, but the Klondike gold miners had cut every tree in the area, built cabins and used the wood for mine supports and firewood. When the wood ran out, they put up tents, so the whole area had been covered with dwellings of every kind, shape and size. Andrew told us that he and his father had built seven cabins here at various times, but now as he looked around, all he could see was scrub willow bushes. The only remaining vestige of history lay in the hundreds, perhaps thousands, of tree stumps around our campsite and as far as the eye could see. Andrew joked that the ones we could see that had been sawn off and not chopped were the ones he cut!

As we sat with late cups of tea, two huge trucks roared past our camp. They were eighteen-wheelers with all the lights on in their cabs and all kinds of decorative and practical road lights around their chassis and on the backs of the trucks. They were quite a sight to see and most of the Gwich'in men had never seen anything like them before. Afterwards, the smell of diesel fumes took a long time to dissipate, and it took us an even longer time to adjust once more to our quiet camp life.

The following day we decided to have a day of rest, take some time to do chores, and give the dogs time to recover from their hard pulling on the gravel road. Some of the men went out to hunt caribou that we had spotted on one of the mountains, while Bill, Andrew, Peter and I went back to Chapman Lake to haul more of our dog feed in. While we were there, a snowplow operator stopped to chat with us, and we got an update on the local geography and distances to various points. He said that he lived in a trailer at a government road-maintenance camp about fifty kilometres to the south and that there was a good place for us to camp across the road from it.

We loaded as much dog feed as we could into our sleds, leaving some to be picked up later, then returned to camp and spent some time fixing our sleds and harnesses ready for the following day. We were all engrossed in our work when a white station wagon pulled to the side of the road beside our camp and out jumped Joe Henry from Dawson City. He was a cousin of William Vittrekwa and an old friend of Andrew Kunnizzi. It was a surprising and happy reunion and they were all off speaking Gwich'in a mile a minute, arms flailing as the old men described our adventures on the trail. As they talked, old William's voice got higher and higher and his toothless mouth seemed to be stuck in a wide grin. It was great to see!

The driver of the car, Ken Snider, said he was the person who was making all the arrangements for our arrival in Dawson. He wanted us to arrive there on March 14 to coincide with the Easter long weekend, and we decided that if we stayed a few days at the government camp, we could do that. However, the men were not eager to hang around for too long, and I told Ken that he was not to take any of them into town before we all went. I was worried that some of them might not get back to us. Ken had brought us some candy bars and a few very welcome sandwiches. M-m-m, white bread for a change! He left at 6:45 after telling us that we had hit the National News on CBC the previous night.

# LEADER OF MEN

Before Inspector Fitzgerald left the camp where constables Kinney and Taylor were to stay, he tied a blue handkerchief to a willow branch to mark the location of the camp. He also left his diary, a notebook and a sack containing some spare duffle socks with the two men.

Fitzgerald and Carter then plodded on down the Peel River. Whether Fitzgerald knew how far gone his men were is unknown, but sometime after he left, twenty-seven-year-old Constable Kinney died. The trip had been impossibly hard, and he was ill from too little of a poor diet, exhaustion and exposure.

One can only imagine how Constable Taylor felt in these circumstances: tired out, hungry, ill and emaciated and now lying in a sleeping bag beside the body of his close friend and partner. A small fire was his only companion. There was no one to talk to, and I wonder if he thought about his family far away to the south. He must have weighed up his alternatives to a long lingering death by freezing and starvation. Perhaps with a last glance at his dead comrade, he picked up his rifle, placed the barrel in his mouth, and with the last of his strength pulled the trigger.

Inspector Fitzgerald and Special Constable Carter walked another sixteen kilometres, bringing them within forty kilometres of Fort McPherson. They were both exhausted as they made their way toward the riverbank. Carter was barely conscious and near to collapse, and he lost his snowshoes as he climbed the bank. Inspector Fitzgerald made a fire and they huddled over it, but within a very short time Carter succumbed to the cold.

Inspector Fitzgerald moved Carter away from the fire, placed his hands on his breast and covered his face with a handkerchief. The inspector must have felt as though the bottom had fallen out of his world. He had been responsible for these men, and even though Carter was at least partially responsible for the circumstances that they had found themselves in, as the commanding officer of the patrol, the inspector bore the ultimate responsibility.

He lay down by the fire and perhaps his thoughts turned to the inevitable end. He was too weak to go on alone and the chances of anyone passing by were too remote to contemplate. He pulled a piece of paper from his pocket and, taking a charred stick from the fire, he wrote, "All money in dispatch bag and bank, clothing, etc., I leave to my beloved mother, Mrs. John Fitzgerald, Halifax. God bless all, F.J. Fitzgerald, RNWMP."

The spirit that had made Inspector Francis Joseph Fitzgerald a leader of men had kept him going on the arduous trail back to Fort McPherson longer than any of his men. But now that spirit was crushed. He placed his will in his pocket and lay down. The sleeping bags had been left with Kinney and Taylor, and he had nothing to pull close around him. A great weariness came over him and the cold ate its way into his starved body. Slowly he lost consciousness and his life ebbed away.

# MOVING ON DOWN THE HIGHWAY

The next morning we continued down the Dempster Highway toward the Highways Department's maintenance camp, stopping on the side of the road at 11:00 for a cup of tea after first parking our dogs over the snowbank in case a truck should come by. Around 2:00 we saw a road marker that told us that we were at mile 42 of the new highway, and at the end of the day when we reached the camp, we found we had covered forty-eight kilometres in six hours, which was quite good going.

When we stopped at the Yukon government road-maintenance

camp, we learned that Yukon time was two hours ahead of Northwest Territories time, a fact that confused us for days after that because our inner clocks took time to adjust. The camp boss, Al Close, told us where we would find a good place to camp. What made it better was that he told us that we could use the camp's dry wood for our stoves, gave us access to fresh water and—what I liked best—access to a shower, complete with hot water. I laughed at William Vittrekwa who said that now he could wash properly and not just "wash his eye."

I was invited for tea at Al's cabin, and as he said he had to make a trip to Dawson, I asked him to send a wire to Muriel in Edmonton to say that all was well and that we were now on the road. When he asked if there was anything else I would like, I gave him a small shopping list that included jam, rice and a bottle of Coca-Cola. Al told us that everyone in the Yukon, and especially in Dawson City, had a nickname and his was "Lugs," and when I looked at him appraisingly, I could see that he did have quite large ears. He laughed when he saw me looking him over and just flipped his ears with his index fingers to acknowledge that I had got the message.

Ken Snider had asked us to wait until the weekend before we came into Dawson, so the next day, after a leisurely breakfast of oats and bacon, I took all of our cooking utensils to the maintenance shop and cleaned them up with some of the camp's dish soap and hot water. Andrew repaired the handle on my teakettle, and I found an empty oil can of suitable size, which when cleaned out gave me a new dog food cooking pot.

In the early afternoon Henry Hanulik and his wife, Barbara, arrived at the maintenance camp, where Henry was employed as the grader and Caterpillar operator. They lived in a trailer close by, and they invited Bill and me there for supper that evening. Barbara said

Travelling down the Dempster Highway in the warm weather was hard on the dogs' feet and made it difficult for them to get snow to quench their thirst.

that when she knew we were coming, she had immediately started to cook apple pies, but when she asked me what I had missed most on the trail, I thought for a few seconds, then told her that I had a sweet tooth and had often thought of lemon meringue pie. When we went to their trailer for supper, she served us a huge meal of excellent sauerkraut and spareribs, and then to my surprise she came out of the kitchen with a huge lemon meringue pie! I was immediately in danger of gaining back the nine kilograms I had lost on the trip. (I weighed myself on their bathroom scale.) We stayed at the Hanuliks' trailer talking until way after 9:00, and when I returned to my tent, I found that William and Andrew were already asleep. Even though the temperature was only minus twelve degrees Celsius, I stoked up the stove and went to bed.

We stayed at the camp for three days, and in spite of the hospitality of the people at the camp, it was quite a strain on all of us. We had not yet arrived at our destination, and in many ways we were eager

The dog teams kept up the pace mile after mile.

to get it over with and get back home, but we realized that the people who were organizing the event at the send-off and arrival points also had agendas that they needed to see accomplished, so we did some more clean-up and maintenance. Three of the men went north with Al to clear the road, and on the way back they rescued the remains of the dog feed from Chapman Lake. The rest of us lazed around, reading magazines from the camp and mending sleds, and I even washed a pair of jeans and sewed the front of my sled with babiche where the moosehide covering on the front curve had split.

In the afternoon I took Mrs. Hanulik for a five-kilometre dog-team ride, and she was quite impressed by the dogs even though I thought that their performance was not 100 percent. I had supper with the Hanuliks, Al Close and Windy Farr. In summer Windy captained the ferry at Dawson, but in winter he worked from the camp steaming out the "glaciers" that formed in the road culverts, so that when the ice melted in the spring, it would not wash out the road.

That evening two White Pass transport trucks came through, hauling aviation fuel to within eighty kilometres of Old Crow. Al said that they were thinking of trucking supplies into the village later in the spring as a winter road already went within five kilometres of it, and they wanted to take advantage of the seismic road that year because it would not be open the following year. It was planned that the Dempster Highway would reach the Ogilvie River in the summer of 1970, but it would be a couple of years after that before it reached Fort McPherson, and it wasn't planned to have a branch going to Old Crow at all. As I listened to him, I thought how incredible it was that things could change so much in such a relatively short time. We had taken twenty-two days to follow old trails for about seven hundred kilometres between McPherson and Dawson, and sixty years ago—within Andrew's and William's lifetimes—Inspector Fitzgerald and his patrol had perished trying to find their way to Dawson City. Now trucks would drive that distance in a matter of hours.

During the night all the dogs began barking, and at 3:30 I finally got up and found that one of William Vittrekwa's dogs was loose. He wasn't a vicious animal so I was able to catch him and tie him up again, but it was hard to get to sleep again and I felt bug-eyed in the morning. The lack of sleep added to my tension and I noted in my diary that "this waiting around doing nothing is pretty hard, even with the excellent hospitality shown us by the folks here."

To work off my frustrations, I borrowed a .22-calibre rifle from Al and, taking my snowshoes with me, walked over six kilometres looking for ptarmigan or rabbits. I came back with one rabbit, which I thought would make a nice change in our diet. When I got back, Henry

I parked my dog sled in front of the road sign commemorating Corporal Dempster's patrol.

Hanulik reported seeing some caribou up the road, so William Teya, Abe Vaneltsi, Henry and I went after them. William Teya shot two caribou, which we hauled back to camp where the other men helped to skin and cut them up. That evening at Bill's request I trimmed his beard, then after some visiting back and forth between the tents I went to bed feeling quite tired.

We left the maintenance camp the next morning while the temperature was reasonably cool, but as soon as the sun came up, the temperature rose to four degrees Celsius. We found that we were facing the sun all the way and what bit of wind there was came from behind us. The dogs found it hard to bite at the hard snow on the roadside and got quite thirsty, so whenever we stopped, they dove over the snowbank at the side of the road and tried to roll in the soft snow beyond, gobbling great mouthfuls of it. We made camp at mile 12, and when Henry and Barbara Hanulik came by in their truck, I went with them as far as the Klondike Highway—surprising two moose on our way there—to see if the promised snowmobile trail had been made. It hadn't, so I changed our plans: we would stay on the main road as far as Chester Henderson's cabin, where we would camp again. On our way back we met a big bull moose, but as we had more than enough meat, we just watched him. He was not at all disturbed by our presence. It's always that way when you don't need the meat.

That day, following the Dempster Road, our patrol covered forty-eight kilometres.

# FINDING THE LOST PATROL

 Superintendent Snyder, the commander of "B" division of the Royal Northwest Mounted Police in Dawson City, became concerned when the patrol from Fort McPherson did not arrive within the allotted time, usually thirty to thirty-five days. He knew that something was really amiss when a group of Gwich'in men arrived and inquired about Inspector Fitzgerald's patrol. They explained that one of their number had been hired by a police patrol to break trail, but he had been paid off after just five days. A few days later another group of Gwich'in arrived and reported that they had seen no sign of the patrol.

Superintendent Snyder sent a message to his headquarters asking for permission to send out a relief patrol, and three days later he received an affirmative answer. As Corporal William John Duncan Dempster had made several trips to Fort McPherson previously, he was chosen to lead the relief patrol. He was given instructions to take two constables and a Gwich'in guide, Charlie Stewart, with him and head for the Hart River Divide to look for Inspector Fitzgerald's trail. Their three teams of five dogs left Dawson City on February 28, 1911, exactly fifty-nine years to the day before our "last patrol" members were reunited on the Peel River after becoming separated the night before. It took Corporal Dempster's relief patrol twelve days to reach the

Little Wind River, having travelled through overflow and deep snow to reach this point.

Searching many of the side creeks took time, but Dempster wanted to make a thorough search in case Fitzgerald had taken a wrong turn. When he and his men stopped to make camp, they stumbled on the remains of an old camping spot littered with empty tins that had held butter and corned beef, and as a clincher they found a piece of flour sack with "RNWMP" stamped on it. The following day they had not travelled very far when they came across another campsite, and Dempster now assumed, because the camps were close together, that Fitzgerald's party had turned back to Fort McPherson. The relief patrol continued, following the old trail, and several days later they came to a cabin where they found an abandoned sled along with its wrapper

Corporal Dempster was sent out from Dawson City with three men to try and locate the Fitzgerald patrol. Dawson City Museum, 1984.222.13.

The Lost Patrol were buried with full military honours in St. Matthews Mission graveyard in Fort McPherson. Dawson City Museum, 1990.78.2.32.

and several sets of dog harnesses. But it was when they discovered dog bones, paws and shoulder blades, which indicated that the dog meat had been eaten, that Dempster understood Inspector Fitzgerald's party had been seriously short of food.

Twenty days after leaving Dawson City Corporal Dempster arrived at Colin Vitsik's cabin on the Peel River, and it was here that Charlie Stewart noticed a dispatch bag and a mail bag in the rafters of the cabin. Now thoroughly alarmed, Corporal Dempster and his men continued on the trail the following day and came at last to a place where there was a tent and poles, a camp stove and some other items, though it didn't look as though it had been an actual camp. Sixteen kilometres farther on they found another toboggan and two sets of dog harnesses out on the river, about ninety metres from the riverbank. The rawhide lashings had all been cut off. As they continued on their way, they began to dread what they would find next.

Corporal Dempster and his men returned to Dawson City after locating the bodies of the men of the Lost Patrol. Dawson City Museum, 2000.183.8.

It was a blue handkerchief that next caught their attention as it fluttered from a willow branch at the river's edge. A trail led up the bank to a small open camp. Two bodies lay side by side. Constable Kinney was easily identified, but the other body was difficult to recognize as Constable Taylor had blown the top off his head—as evidenced by the hands that still gripped the rifle. In the ashes of a fire sat a kettle, and in it were strips of rawhide that had been boiled in a final attempt for the men to get some nourishment. Underneath the frozen bodies Dempster found a sack with spare duffles in it, a notebook and a diary that had been left by Inspector Fitzgerald.

Reading the diary must have filled the relief expedition with horror. These men had been their colleagues and they probably knew each other well. Corporal Dempster would have realized that what they had found was going to cause shockwaves not only in the police force but around the world as well. However, he still had to find the other two men, and after covering the two bodies with brush, the patrol continued on its way. At this point Fort McPherson was only forty-eight kilometres away, and Dempster must have been cautiously optimistic that Fitzgerald and Carter had made it back to the village. But if they had, why had no one come to recover the bodies of the other two policemen?

Just sixteen kilometres down the river from the place where they had found the two constables' bodies, Corporal Dempster noticed a trail leading to the riverbank, and as they approached the site, they stumbled on a pair of snowshoes. At the top of the bank their fears were realized when they found the bodies of Inspector Fitzgerald and Special Constable Carter. They could see that Carter had died first because he had been moved from beside the fire, his arms had been crossed on his chest and a handkerchief covered his face. No attempt had been made to set up camp and there were no signs of any dogs. Corporal Dempster could tell by the bodies that the men were starved and had succumbed to the cold. They covered the bodies with brush, as they had done for the other two men, and then travelled on to Fort McPherson, where they arrived at 6:00 that night.

When Corporal Dempster reported the tragedy to the officer in command, there was the expected shock, which soon spread throughout the community. The officer explained that since Fitzgerald had planned to stay in Dawson before going on to the coronation, no one had worried about his whereabouts. As the RNWMP detachment in Fort McPherson did not own any dogs, and Inspector Fitzgerald had commandeered all the dogs but one to make his patrol, it was now necessary to borrow dog teams from the Anglican Mission and from John Firth at the Hudson's Bay store so that the bodies of the Lost Patrol could be brought to the village.

And so it was that the next morning the bodies were brought into Fort McPherson and a military funeral was arranged.

# DAWSON AT LAST

Our patrol set off for our last few days on the trail, but we soon stopped at the junction where the Dempster joins the Klondike Highway. We had to smile at the large signs—glaring red letters on a white background—that had been erected at strategic points on the highway warning drivers to "Watch for Dog Teams!" Then we gathered at the sign at the junction that described Corporal Dempster's relief patrol, and I took several photographs for the record.

Warning signs were placed on the Klondike Highway to warn truck drivers that dog teams would be coming off the Dempster Highway.

Dawson City, the "City of Gold," with the Midnight Dome as a backdrop, welcomed us as we came into the city across the Klondike River bridge.

The temperature was minus twenty degrees Celsius when we had left camp, which wasn't a bad temperature for the dogs to work in, but again there was gravel on the highway which made it difficult for the dogs to pull the sleds, so we ran behind our sleds to try to make the going a bit easier. After we had been travelling for a time, a pick-up truck stopped and the driver told me that William Vittrekwa—he didn't give William's name, but when he described him, I knew that it was my old friend William—was having trouble with his dogs and that Bill Antaya had gone back to help him. By the time Bill got there, William had shot one of his dogs, which by all accounts had hemoptysis, or what the Gwich'in described as "breaking his wind." It is a condition that occurs when a dog has strained so much at pulling that his lungs have hemorrhaged and filled with blood; it is invariably fatal. William,

We drove our teams into the city feeling on top of the world.

not wanting to see his dog suffer, had shot him. Afterwards he told me it was as if he had shot himself because the dog had worked so hard and brought him all this way only to die before reaching our destination. William was quite upset and I could see how close he was to his dogs, though these were work dogs and not pets, and it was unusual to see him regard his dogs as friends. I had never seen him abuse his dogs and they were very obedient to him.

We made camp near a cabin belonging to Chester Henderson, and after we were settled, we went to visit him. Chester, who was one of Dawson City's "characters," had an awesome collection of axes and axe heads, all brand new. He said that he had been cutting wood for a living for twenty years or more and usually cut 150 cords of green wood every year, taking it into Dawson for sale. We sat and talked with him about his life and work and in turn told him of our trip. After a relaxing evening we returned to our camp and turned in early as we were all tired and looked forward to the day when we would at last enter Dawson City. We had travelled forty kilometres on the highway that day.

We broke camp for the last time on Friday, March 13, 1970, twenty-six days after leaving Fort McPherson. This included five days off for one reason or another, most of that delay being the time spent at the Dempster maintenance camp. I noted that the fastest time for any patrol between those two settlements was fourteen days, a record set by Corporal Dempster some years after the Lost Patrol incident. Inspector Fitzgerald had expected to make the trip in less than thirty days.

After a good breakfast of hotcakes and oatmeal, we packed all our possessions into our sleds, dressed our dogs up in their fancy blankets and straightened the dog irons. Then we donned our caribou-skin parkas and Centennial hats, which we had kept in the sleds until this last day. The plan was for William Vittrekwa to lead us into Dawson, but his dogs were a bit too slow, and we began piling up behind him. Then Bill got bitten by some dogs that came too close to him, and shortly afterwards Abe Vaneltsi was bitten, too. At that point, in order to move things along, I went out in front, and though I was a bit worried that my team would make a mess of things and misbehave, they behaved splendidly. I was so pleased with my lead dog, Silver—he had started the trip so slowly with his injured leg, but now he paced out in front without a care in the world and not only listened to my commands but obeyed them, too.

We drove our teams through Bear Creek, which was a "ghost village," and saw quite a few houses but no residents. In fact, it was here that a red fox shot across the trail, and I thought that my dogs were going to take off after it, but after quickening their

The dogs took us to the monument dedicated to Inspector Fitzgerald, which was located on the front grounds of the RCMP barracks where people were given the opportunity for a photo op.

pace for a moment, they soon
settled down again. We came to
the mouth of Bonanza Creek,
where gold was first discovered
in 1896, and here we were met
by a police cruiser, which es-
corted us into Dawson City. We
came in a long procession along
the main street, which runs par-
allel to the Yukon River, and as
we passed the old folks' home,
we could see people on the bal-
cony watching us and waving.
Later I was told that one old

As a representative of the members of the patrol I was given the key to the City of Dawson by Mayor Fabien Salois.

man had watched us go by with tears in his eyes; he said that he had not
seen dog teams in Dawson since the 1920s and never expected to see
them again. We were pleased that we had brought some good memo-
ries to life for him. The main street was crowded with well-wishers
who had come to welcome us, and I am sure that we were popular with
the schoolchildren because they had all been given the day off.

We were led to the RCMP detachment, which featured a monument in memory of Inspector Fitzgerald and his men in the front yard.
As I called for Silver to turn into the police yard, a small dog that was
tethered to a clothesline shot out in front of us, took one look at the
dogs advancing on him and shot back into the yard, up the steps and
onto the porch of the house. A woman quickly opened the door to
retrieve her little pooch, but I had great difficulty keeping my dogs
from entering the kitchen after it. Order was soon restored, and I led
the teams into the detachment yard where we lined up and had photographs taken. We went from there to the Federal Building where the

mayor, Fabien Salois, made a speech welcoming us to Dawson, and I was presented with a huge golden key with a ribbon of Yukon tartan attached to it. On behalf of all the Dempster Patrol members, I accepted this key symbolizing the freedom of the City of Dawson. Andrew Kunnizzi and Fred Vittrekwa then handed the sack of mail that we had carried to Dawson City's postmaster, Frank Lidstone. The sack contained over two hundred letters, some of which were destined for dignitaries and friends around the world beginning with the governors general of all the countries in the Commonwealth.

After travelling twenty-four kilometres on our last day, for a total of 764 kilometres over the entire trip, we drove our dogs down to the Yukon River, where stakes had been frozen into the river ice for us. We fastened our sixty-six dogs there, with thirty-five on one side and thirty-one on the other side of a cleared ice road in the middle of the river, and it was quite a sight to see. We fed them well and made

Our tired dogs were taken to the Yukon River and tied up to posts frozen into the river for us. Citizens were warned to keep their pets tied up so our dogs would not attack them.

a fuss of them, then went back into Dawson where a "Welcome to Dawson" reception tea was held. Percy Henry, the chief of the Dawson Band, made a speech in the Takudh language and welcomed us all into his territory. William Vittrekwa responded by saying that the people had been worried "about these old men coming." Then he

Ninety-year-old ex-guide Richard Martin, who was now blind, presented this sign to the people of Fort McPherson from the people of Dawson City.

continued: "If I die, I will be buried there [indicating the mountains], but if I make it to Dawson City, my name will be big when I die, and now I am here I am very happy to be here in the City of Gold!" Abe Vaneltsi, our youngest patrol member, said that "the older men camped by themselves, and the younger men camped together and it was a very sociable trip." He said that he had walked so far through snow, brush and willows "that my singing snowshoes just about burned up!" Abe had celebrated his twenty-first birthday out on the trail.

In the evening a banquet and dance was held in our honour, sponsored by the Territorial government, and more than a hundred guests attended. Following the meal, a number of presentations were made, and a senior representative of the Game Department said that Andrew, at seventy-eight years, and William, who was "only" seventy-seven, were eight feet tall for their achievement, "and not many people would be able to do this even at our age!" He went on to say that the rest of us were seven feet eleven inches for our participation. He then presented us all with Yukon bolo ties. We were also presented with gold-plated

Not to be outdone, Chief Henry of the Dawson Trondek Hwich'in Band presented a plaque to the Tetlit Gwich'in of Fort McPherson.

Dawson Dollars on a Yukon Tartan medallion holder, and the Yukon Order of Pioneers made us honorary members of the association and gave us a book about the life of Jack McQuesten, the founder of the Lodge. Afterwards an orchestra provided music for a dance, and one of the funniest sights was during a modern dance: everyone was gyrating around with their partners, and there was Andrew Kunnizzi just having the time of his life gyrating like the best of them without a partner. I don't think anyone noticed in the general melee.

At the dance, the government representatives from both the Yukon and the Northwest Territories took the opportunity to have their say. Mayor Fabien Salois presented a trophy from the people of the Yukon to Chief John Tetlichi, who was there both as chief of the First Nations in Fort McPherson and as the councillor for the Delta on the Northwest Territories Council. He had flown with the other dignitaries from Fort McPherson to welcome us because we were from his village, and he was quite proud of the patrol's accomplishment. Then

Alex Gordon, the assistant director of the Mackenzie Delta Region for the NWT government, drew attention to the aim of the Centennial celebrations of fostering a greater sense of unity in the North and showed the special symbol on the centennial flags that depicted First Nations, Inuit and white men and women working together.

The people of Dawson presented us with a huge wooden sign, a metre and a half square, which we were to take back to the people of Fort McPherson. It featured a large, circular "City of Dawson" crest carved into the bottom right-hand corner, the work of Lil Munroe of Dawson.

The sign read:

Commemorating the Fort McPherson NWT Centennial '70 project Feb 16–March 14. Eleven Dog teams travelled from here to Dawson City via the RNWMP Dawson Patrol route (established following gold rush times). Anticipating that soon the Dempster Highway will link our two communities.

Although our actual route was different from that described on the sign, the sentiment was right. Richard Martin, then in his ninetieth year and blind since 1927, then spoke about the time before the patrols. He had made many patrols with his brother, and told us that we had taken his old trail. Then for our benefit he explained again that the route we had taken was for those who didn't mind climbing mountains and who were travelling light. Not to be outdone by all the presentations, the Dawson Band had prepared an equally impressive sign with the Yukon crest at the centre and these words carved on the left-hand side:

Mussi Cho (a big thank you) for your eleven mushers and teams reliving the "Dawson Patrol" in NWT Centennial, first major project. Feb 16–Mar 14.

On the right hand side was carved:

Remembering hunting grounds shared, friendships that last forever and hoping to see Peel River people more often.

P. Henry: Chief Dawson Band.

We were royally wined and dined by the good people of that famed city of gold, then given a tour of the city and the surrounding area. Then at last we retired to our hotel rooms, which were provided by the City of Dawson. We ate all our meals at Black Mike's café—all courtesy of the city.

The men had a very good time, although one or two probably didn't know if they had a good time or not. One of our men came out of a bar totally inebriated, and as I passed him, he collapsed and I was able to catch him, sling him over my shoulder, carry him to his hotel

Dogs and men, along with all the equipment, were flown back to Fort McPherson in a DC3, where it was quickly unloaded along with our "Freedom of the City" key.

room and dump him on his bed. But in spite of a few things like this, no one got into trouble. One morning we all met in Ken Snider's house for a late breakfast while Ken was trying to get hold of CBC Radio to do an interview with us. I was a bit relieved when he couldn't get through.

It was several days before we were ready to leave. The dogs were to be driven out to the airport, and as Bill and I were going to be driving out there in a rental car, we took some of my dogs with us while the rest would be driven out in a truck. I am sure that Silver, my lead dog, thought that this was too good to be true, and he rode all the way out there with his nose out the window.

The reality of progress was forced upon us when we climbed

I think even the dogs were thankful for the free ride home.

aboard the DC-3 aircraft that was to take us back to Fort McPherson. It took two flights to get all the men, the dogs and our equipment back home, and as we loaded the first six teams, we left the dogs in their harnesses so that we could control them better. The last thing we wanted was a dogfight as we flew over the mountains! Just before takeoff the pilot came to the cockpit door to check on us and cried, "Hold it! I can't believe what I am seeing! I just have to get a photograph of this. I'll never get the same kind of load ever again!" He took a photograph of our six teams, still in harness and all lined up in the plane with our sleds attached, and beside them six men, each of us holding a big stick to quell any bad tempers. The dogs were a bit snarly because of the close proximity of other dogs, but once the plane's engines were revved up they just lay quietly and enjoyed the ride.

We glanced out of the windows at the mountains and the creeks that we had been travelling down just a short time ago. We had been on the trail for twenty-one days to reach Dawson City, and the flight back to Fort McPherson took just two and a half hours. It was plain to see why the RNWMP had ceased making patrols by dog team.

When the plane landed on the Peel River ice at Fort McPherson, I was tired but still excited, and more than anything I was proud to have been part of the patrol.

Opposite: Bill Antaya and William Vittrekwa prepare to climb out of the second DC3, thankful to be home.

# A STUNNING LOSS

 As expected, the members of the RNWMP were stunned by the news of what quickly became known as the Lost Patrol, and as the details emerged of how the men of the patrol had made tremendous efforts to return to their base with the odds stacked against them, and how they had been denied success so close and yet so far from home, there was great sorrow. Corporal Dempster reported that all the bodies were extremely emaciated and all—with the exception of Taylor—had died from exposure and starvation. Not one body was thought to have weighed over forty-five kilograms.

The age of adventure and exploration was nearing an end, but while we cannot put the clocks back to 1911, for a short period of time back in 1970 eleven men and sixty-seven dogs paid tribute to those pioneers who blazed overland trails in an inhospitable land. Now hundreds of tourists travel the Dempster Highway every year, and as they pass the graveyard in Fort McPherson, they can see, surrounded by a chain, the white headstones that mark the graves of the men of the Lost Patrol.

# UNEXPECTED SOUVENIR

To my great disappointment a plane was ready and able to take me to Inuvik the same night that we all got back to Fort McPherson, and since it was a freebie seat, I could not afford to turn it down. I only had a very brief time to visit with the men and my Fort McPherson hosts before climbing into the small plane, something that bothered me for a long time afterwards. You cannot live in close proximity to ten men, sharing food and fire with them for twenty-odd days, without feeling a kinship with them, and to leave abruptly did not seem right.

As I was leaving, Dave Sullivan asked me if I would like a husky pup to take home as a souvenir. To push the point, he said that the pup's mother had more pups than she could feed and he would have to put one or two down if he couldn't interest anyone in taking them. I looked at the pup. She had beautiful markings but her eyes were still closed! How could I know anything about her without seeing her eyes? "If you take this baby bottle, you can feed her. I'll fill it with milk," Helen said appealingly. "Just look how sweet she is!"

Without really thinking of the consequences, I took the pup, wrapped her up and put her in my pocket. I got to Inuvik, stayed at the hospital residence again, put the pup in a small cardboard box and made arrangements to catch the mainliner to Edmonton the next morning.

But wait a minute, could I take a pup on board a commercial airliner?

The next day I called a taxi and went out to the airport carrying my equipment—snowshoes, rifle, winter sleeping bag—and all my winter clothes stuffed into a kit bag, the small pup once again in my pocket. The people at the counter didn't turn a hair at the amount of equipment I had and calmly put everything through the baggage check. I kept silent about my pup. All went well until about an hour into the flight when the pup started squirming, and I knew that I had to feed her. I was sitting alone in the row, and when the flight attendant came by, I held the bottle out and asked her if she could warm it for me. She looked a bit surprised but took it, and a short time later she came back, handed it to me and then just stood there. I looked up at her, holding the bottle in my hand. She smiled as only a stewardess can and said, "I'm waiting here because I want to know what you're going to do with it!" I realized what a crazy situation I was in: she didn't really think I was going to guzzle it down myself, did she? I gently extricated my pup (which we named Tanya when I got home) from my pocket. Fortunately the sight must have brought out all the attendant's maternal feelings because she sat down, declared the pup was "adorable" and all the other cuddly adjectives and asked how I had got it and where I had been. As I told her my story, she asked if I would mind if she fed the pup. When she was done, she re-wrapped the pup in a paper towel (Tanya wasn't housebroken yet), and then said that she would like to take her to show the pilots. That was about the last I saw of my pup until we were landing in Edmonton, where I had to explain this "little bundle of joy" to my wife. But I wasn't the only one to spring a surprise because my wife had driven through Edmonton to pick me up—when I left for Fort McPherson, she couldn't drive!

It was difficult to adjust to sleeping in a soft bed again and the house seemed incredibly hot. I'm sure it was an adjustment for my wife, too.

No one else would ever make a dog-team patrol as the men from Fort McPherson had done it: the Dempster Highway would see to that. It was the end of an era. In 1995 the RCMP made a centennial trip on the old route to mark one hundred years of the force's presence in the Yukon, but they did it on snowmobiles, and the dog team that accompanied them was an Alaskan-style sled and team. Now tourists travel the Dempster Highway, the "Last Adventure Highway in North America." It is a unique trip where the snow still flies at any time of the year and the winds howl so that, if you close your eyes and listen, you can picture the men with their heads bowed into the blizzard as they battle the storm.

# EPILOGUE

The Last Patrol project made quite an impact on the village of Fort McPherson, but it was certainly not the last notable event in the Northwest Territories. Another ten years went by before the Dempster Highway was completed and opened, but in that time the Gwich'in people of the North became known for other feats of strength and perseverance. Sharon and Shirley Firth of Aklavik became world-famous cross-country skiers, members of Canada's cross-country team for seventeen consecutive years, travelling to four Olympic Games and between them winning seventy-nine medals in national championships. Canoeists from Fort McPherson paddled in the wake of Mackenzie and others explorers throughout the Northwest Territories and British Columbia and in 1967 participated in the Canadian Centennial canoe race from Rocky Mountain House to Montreal, paddling over 5,200 kilometres. Annual snowmobile excursions were organized to Old Crow and back, following the traditional trails through the Richardson Mountains. A snowmobile trip to Mayo was made so that visits between old friends of Gwich'in ancestry could be encouraged, and finally the Gwich'in people themselves have taken full control of their village and land.

In the year 2013 only two members of the Last Patrol survive. Now in his seventies, Abe Koe still lives in Fort McPherson and visits his fish camp every year. He also does some trapping and otherwise stays active. The author, Keith Billington, lives with his wife in Prince

George, BC, where they both cross-country ski in winter and find adventure in their sea kayak in summer if they are not travelling or hiking in some remote area. Keith enjoys writing about their exploits.

Seven members of the Last Patrol are buried in the same Fort McPherson graveyard where Inspector Fitzgerald and his men lie in the permafrost. Another member of the patrol was presumed drowned, though his body was never located, and one member, Bill Antaya, died back in his home on the Prairies.

These are the stories of the North, where people endure cold and hardship during their adventures. Each member of the Last Patrol, true Northerners all, faced life with resolution and determination right to the end.

# ACKNOWLEDGEMENTS

This book could not have been written if I had not been closely associated with the Gwich'in people of Fort McPherson who taught me about living in the North.

A special mention is made of the men who accompanied me on the Dawson Patrol: The late Andrew Kunnizzi, William Vittrekwa, George Robert, Abraham Vaneltsi, Peter Nerysoo, William Teya, Jim Vittrekwa, Fred Vittrekwa and Bill Antaya. My good friend Abraham Koe still talks regularly to me about our trip.

We appreciated the wonderful skills of the women who spent many hours sewing our authentic clothing and making us proud to represent Fort McPherson.

The Firths, Sullivans, Hanuliks, Sniders and the people of Dawson City were generous and caring and all deserve mention, and to the families we left behind when we set out on a re-enactment of a tragic trip, we owe thanks for the confidence, love and support they gave us.

# INDEX